# ANYTHING FOR
# A QUIET LIFE

# ANYTHING FOR A QUIET LIFE

*the autobiography of*
JACK HAWKINS

*with a postscript by*
DOREEN HAWKINS

STEIN AND DAY/*Publishers*/New York

PN
2598
H 346
A 3
1974

First published in The United States of America by
Stein and Day/*Publishers* in 1974.
Copyright © 1973 by Mrs. Doreen Hawkins and the
estate of the late Jack Hawkins
Library of Congress Catalog Card No. 74-78527
All rights reserved
Printed in the United States of America
Stein and Day/*Publishers*/Scarborough House, Briarcliff Manor, N.Y. 10510
ISBN 0-8128-1708-7

For
Nick, Andy and Caroline
from
the Old Man

# CONTENTS

# LIST OF ILLUSTRATIONS

15 1953—early days at Roehampton, with Nick aged five (aloft) and Andy, two.

16 At a Royal Première in November 1954 at the Empire, Leicester Square. Nick was to present the bouquet to the Queen.

17 1955, when Nick was seven and fishing a great passion.

18 As Major Warden in *The Bridge on the River Kwai* (1957).

19 *League of Gentlemen* (1960). At the back, camera-man Arthur Ibbetson, director Basil Dearden and myself. On the left, Terence Alexander, Norman Bird and Keiron Moore. On the right, Bryan Forbes, Roger Livesey and Richard Attenborough, and at the front Nigel Patrick.

20 Receiving the *Ben-Hur* award from the Duke of Edinburgh in 1960.

21 The winter of 1962, with Andrew (twelve), Caroline (eight) and Nick (thirteen).

22 The day I left London's University College Hospital, 10 February 1966.

23 With Nick, working on a film in Africa (October 1971).

24 With Dee at the première of *The Ruling Class* (1972) of which I was a co-producer.

# ANYTHING FOR
# A QUIET LIFE

# ONE

Looking back, the scene seems both bizarre and ironic, but at the time it was just another item in another working day. One of my oldest friends, Raymond Massey—and Richard Chamberlain—both dressed in the crisp white coats of surgeons, stood looking down at me as I lay tucked up in a hospital bed. Their faces expressed grave concern, as well they might, for I was dying.

Beautiful nurses hovered efficiently in the background, and massive arc lights burned down on the three of us with a bright and shadowless intensity.

On the dark perimeter of this bright pool of light I could make out the familiar figures of technicians in windcheaters and jeans, and the cameras gliding smoothly and silently on their tracks. By courtesy of the make-up artists my face was the grey, drawn portrait of a man close to death. I opened my mouth to say what was expected of me at this sombre moment—and for the first time in my life my voice deserted me.

'It's no good, I can hardly speak,' I croaked in a wholly un-scripted line, simply stating a fact. The others looked surprised, and the director joined the group round my bed.

'Don't worry, Jack,' he said reassuringly. 'You're great. Your voice sounds just like a man who has suffered a bad heart attack.'

In fact, I had suffered something infinitely worse for an actor; I had lost the power of speech.

He could not guess—and nor could I—that, within a few weeks, I would be lying in another identical hospital bed, but far away from the paraphernalia of a film studio, and in a real hospital, knowing that as an actor who lives by his voice, I was as surely dead as if I had been struck down by a massive heart attack.

Looking back to that day in bed in a Hollywood studio filming an episode for the *Dr Kildare* TV series, I suppose this was the moment when I had to admit the previously inadmittable; that what I had feared for the past five years, had refused to accept, and had covered up continually by making excuses to myself, was an irreversible fact: I had cancer of the throat.

Cancer is so malignant, so cruelly and destructively greedy as it gnaws and destroys, that it is almost impossible to accept that you can be suffering from this most dread of all diseases. You speak in hushed tones about friends and relatives who have suffered from the grip of cancer, for it is always someone else who suffers from it, never you yourself.

'Not me,' you assure yourself. 'This can't happen to me.' But it can, and it did, and it does.

I had been reassuring myself continually since I had first been treated for a secondary condition of the larynx, that caused me trouble while I was making *League of Gentlemen* in 1959. Despite the depressing feeling that this was now recurring, I struggled on with the *Dr Kildare* filming, all the time fighting to prevent my voice from fading out altogether—and ironically delighting the production company with my realistic performance of a desperately ill man. No one had any inkling of my own inward private fears, of course, and still less of my own medical condition, and to add to the surrealism of the whole situation, I was offered a leading part in a new television series to be made in Hollywood.

To me, this seemed a particularly silly idea, when the producers knew my voice was hoarse. It was rather like selecting a one-legged hurdler for an Olympic team, for making a twenty-six-part TV series is a tough relentless job and no place for the weak or weary, but then Hollywood has a happy knack of ignoring the impossible.

'Don't worry,' I was told. 'You will be fine,' and the producer made me an offer which, as they say in the Mafia, I couldn't refuse. Their optimism that my throat trouble was something very simple and unimportant was like a tonic to me, and it was also shared by two Beverly Hills throat specialists I consulted. They both examined me, prescribed some minor treatment—a mouth-wash and an antiseptic gargle—and assured me that I had nothing to worry about.

This chorus of confidence lulled my own belief about my condition—after all, who was I to argue with two specialists of renown?—and I looked forward to the first day's shooting with that peculiar and exhilarating feeling of tense excitement that always comes with the start of a new production, for every new part is a fresh challenge, and without challenge of some kind life loses its savour.

This was a totally false frame of mind, because since I had seen the two specialists (and despite their treatment) I had been suffering increasingly from pain in my throat. This finally grew so severe that I went to see another doctor at the University of California Hospital, and asked his opinion. He was non-committal, and suggested that I should come into the hospital for a thorough check-up. This was a sensible proposal, but there is something very heady in being acclaimed as a star in Hollywood. I was in demand, and this gave me an excuse that was very convenient.

'I'm sorry, but I can't come in just yet,' I told him. 'I've got to be ready for the first day's shooting of a new television series tomorrow.'

'In that case, I wish you good luck,' the doctor said, and we shook hands. Even this reassured me; after all, if he had thought I had cancer, he would have whipped me in at once, wouldn't he?

So, lulled by wishful thinking, I drove from my hotel early to the studios on a glorious Californian morning. It was the kind of morning when you feel you can tackle anything with pleasure, even tedious hours in make-up and the wardrobe department. The air was fresh, the sun felt warm, and as someone who feels particularly alert and at ease in a warm climate, I felt convinced that all was right with my world.

When I walked out on to the studio floor to play my first scene, I was still feeling pleased with life, but after the first few lines I suddenly felt my voice weakening. It faded like a radio when the battery runs down, and by the end of the scene I was struggling to speak normally.

3

By the second scene, my voice had faded to a horrible, hoarse whisper. The director came over to me. It was clear that he did not quite know what to say or do. Here, on the second scene of the first day's shooting of a long and tiring schedule, the star had lost his voice. He had no idea what the trouble might be, but it was sufficient it was there. After all, he had a whole cast to consider, location hotels booked, and an intricate jig-saw of dates for weeks and weeks ahead. The company stood to lose thousands of dollars for each day they fell behind on the programme of shooting. They could not afford illness. None of these worries showed on his face.

'Look, Jack,' he said easily. 'You go to your dressing-room and have a rest. We'll give you a call when we need you back on the set.'

I thankfully went to my room, poured myself a large drink, and sat down. I thumbed through the script, and learned some lines. An hour passed. And then another. No one called me, and somehow I knew that no one would. All day I waited, and then, when everyone else had gone home, I returned to my hotel. I had not shot one frame of film, and I knew that I never would, either. The chips were down, my bluff was called: an actor without a voice is as much use in a studio as a camera without film.

That evening, the specialist I had seen at the University Hospital called to see me. It was obvious that the film company had sent him to discover what was wrong and how long it would take to cure, if it could be cured. He was gentle and considerate.

'I do wish you would let me give you a thorough check-out,' he said.

Well, I had been through all this before in England. I had been put under an anaesthetic and had my larynx scraped; I had been subject to endless tests, and I had undergone cobalt treatment to the point when it would have been fatal for me to have received any more.

'I'm sorry,' I told him. 'But I am going home. If anything drastic is going to happen, I would rather it took place in London.'

He quite understood.

The next day, I flew back to Britain, and within a few hours of

4

touching down at Heathrow, I was being put through a pathological examination at University Hospital in London. Altogether, the tests took two days. These were days blurred by feelings of fear and resignation and mercifully dulled by ignorance of what was really happening to me, beyond the certain fact that I faced a terrible and overwhelming change in my life.

The final act remains very clearly in my memory. Doreen, my wife, was sitting in the armchair, and I was perched on the bed, when the surgeon came into the room. We had not been saying much to each other; it hurt me too much to talk, anyway.

I had been in hospital for two days, undergoing tests. Now the surgeon had come to tell us what the results of those tests were. There was a benign expression on his face. But that told one nothing, because he always had a benign air about him.

'I'm so sorry to have kept you waiting,' he said, 'but the pathologist's final report has only just come in.'

I knew what he was going to say. This was the punch-line of all the dialogue that had been going on for some time; the punch-line that one didn't want to hear, and yet that one knew, in one's heart of hearts, had to be spoken and heard. Fortunately, he didn't muff it, and I was grateful for that.

'There is a definite malignancy of the larynx,' he said directly.

Still neither Dee nor I spoke. The silence roared at us.

'Why don't you go home and talk it over?' Mr Formby suggested. 'Then let me know.'

I looked at Dee. She was calmness personified, but in her eyes there was a pleading. The alternatives were clear-cut; silence and life, speech and a quick death.

'What is there to discuss?' I croaked. 'When will you do it?'

'I'll let you know,' he said.

We went out to the car. The chauffeur opened the door, and we drove home in silence, both too deep in our own thoughts to speak. And, after all, what was there to say?

To make matters worse, it was the Christmas holidays, with our three children home from school, and the Christmas decorations still up.

We had a drink, dinner with the children and went to bed. What else to do?

My understanding of a laryngectomy—the operation I faced—was fairly sketchy, but I did know that it involved the removal of the larynx, the cavity in the throat that contains the vocal cords, and the 'voice box'. When the larynx is removed, the windpipe is severed and grafted to a hole made in the wall of the throat, about the size of a ten-penny piece, through which the patient breathes. All sense of smell is lost, but, much more important, so is the conventional means of speech. For a normal person this is grave enough, but for an actor it is a sentence of working death. For how can a man who lives by the spoken word make a living if he cannot speak?

But decisions like this cannot be taken solely with one's own interests at heart. If I let my actor-selfishness get the better of me—and it was tempting, despite the pain—the few months of life I would have left might be acceptable to me, but what about the permanent absence which would follow my death; what effect would that have on the lives of those I loved and who loved me?

Yet, even as these thoughts formulated themselves they raised other doubts. What right had one to imagine that one meant so much to even one other person that she would miss you—and be unhappy—if you were not there? One may love with totality; but has one the right to expect to be loved totally in return?

We live in a confused human situation; whatever one does can be interpreted as self-interest.

But, thank God, Dee knew what she wanted—a voiceless me, so long as I lived and breathed. That made the decision, when it came, easier. It took all the responsibility away from me, and became a decision made for me, but which I could con myself was my own. Actor I might be, but even a voiceless life held far more than the silence of death. And I could console myself that it was love that persuaded me to take the final step. Whose love, and for whom, was beside the point.

Next morning was black. I lasted out until midday, then had my secretary telephone the surgeon's.

6

'Mr Hawkins must be patient . . . he must realise that the theatre has to be booked, anaesthetist engaged, theatre sisters available. . . .'

I don't remember much about the next two days, except that the pestering of the surgeon's secretary went on. This was not the courage of wanting to get it over and done with; it was cowardice pure and simple; I was terrified by the waiting; terrified of time in which to think; terrified of being tempted to retract.

Then at last came the message. 'Would Mr Hawkins report to the hospital on Friday evening? Mr Formby would operate on Saturday afternoon.'

Dee drove me to the hospital. Even in the midst of tragedy, there is always humour. Dee was driving me down Putney Hill when a car rushed out of a side road and made her swerve.

Infuriated, I wound down my window and miraculously recovered my full stage voice to shout: 'You bastard!' I shouted so loudly that the words echoed from the walls. It was ironic that they should, for these were the last words I uttered in my own voice.

At the hospital we had a gentle half-bottle of champagne and she left with a smiling, see-you-tomorrow wave.

Before dawn, so it seemed, a crackling white-gowned character brought me a cup of tea.

'It's the last refreshment you'll get for a LONG time,' she announced with kindly malice. Then laughed: 'The barber will be along presently.'

'That's good,' I said, rubbing my hand across the stubble on my chin.

She saw my gesture, and said with mock seriousness: 'Oh, no, Mr Hawkins. Nipples to knees.'

'To knees!' I exclaimed, shattered at the thought of so much nakedness. 'But it's my throat that's being cut.'

'Now, don't be naughty, Mr Hawkins,' she chided me for my sick attempt at a joke.

Presently the barber came. He was a nice little man, smooth like an undertaker. With serious pride in his work, he soaped, with a non-lathering soap, the fourteen hairs on my chest. At his

7

first stroke, he removed three of them, and a sizeable piece of skin.

'Under the arms, too, I think, nurse?'

The nurse nodded, and the pre-war blade got to work again. In the days to come these shaven areas were to prove the most uncomfortable cuts of all.

After a brief lull, suddenly my room seemed as crowded as the transit lounge at London Airport. A nurse appeared with 'pre-med' pills, or something; a second swept in with an enormous pair of woollen socks, obviously left-overs from some Arctic expedition, and deftly put my legs in them—'I say, it can't be that cold in the theatre!'

She gave me a thin smile. 'You'd be surprised!' And yet a third came, took away my newspapers and put them on the dressing-table. 'Now, lie quiet and relax,' she admonished.

When the door had closed behind her, I retrieved my news-papers. But I was not left in peace for long. Back she came, and with her two strapping orderlies pulling an elongated dessert trolley, on to which they unceremoniously loaded me, wheeled me out into the corridor. As we went I was vaguely aware of figures attending my Royal Progress. I gave them what I hoped was a regal wave.

Into the lift—button pushed—silent, and, for my liking, too rapid descent. Too soon we were in the foyer of the theatre.

Smiling reassurance, the genial anaesthetist applied a tourniquet to my arm, and with professional seriousness congratulated me on having a fine upstanding vein.

'You'll feel a slight jab, and I want you to count up to ten,' he said.

On previous occasions I had never got beyond three and a half. But I wouldn't argue. Anything for a quiet life!

'Now, sing this SCALE for me.'

The voice of the Man of God, and the scene transformed from the hospital theatre to the vestry of St Michael's, the parish church of Wood Green, in north London.

'Now, sing THIS scale for me,' repeated the Vicar, the Rev. Mr Midwinter, striking another chord.

I was barely eight years old, and here I was taking part in a voice trial for the church choir.

'Sing the middle note of these three.'

'Good. Now the bottom note of these.'

'Read the 23rd Psalm for me.'

'. . . and lead me forth beside the waters of comfort. He shall . . .'

'Thank you, my boy. What's your favourite hymn? Like to sing a couple of verses for me?'

Later the Vicar called with the news that I had been successful, and I took my place in the choir stalls as the most junior boy on Decani.

As I floated away on the mists of oblivion, I was aware of myself trilling away to his approving nods; of being instructed to repeat the lovely reassuring words of the 23rd Psalm. Quite clearly I heard myself say: '. . . He leadeth me beside the still waters . . . Yea, though I walk through the valley of the shadow of death . . . I will fear no evil . . .'

# TWO

My birth on 14th September 1910 was more than just an ordinary event in my parents' terraced house in Lyndhurst Road, Wood Green, London.

In the family, I was always referred to as 'the after-thought', because I am sure I came as a surprise to my parents, since they believed they had completed their family with the birth of my brother Tom, ten years before. By the time I appeared, my sisters, Gladys and Florence, were already in their teens.

Being the youngest by such a wide margin, I was thoroughly indulged, but in affection rather than in material things, for although my father was a respected master builder, who made most of his living out of local authority contracts, we were by no means wealthy, and there was little money to spare on luxuries.

Wood Green in those days was a quiet, almost remote suburb. The tradesmen delivered their goods—milk, bread, coal—from horse-drawn carts, and life in our road was as ordered and untroubled as a country village. Both my widowed grandmothers lived near by; Grandma Hawkins in a house filled with massive Victorian furniture and a succession of married and unmarried children, and Grandma Goodman, my mother's mother, sadly alone, and with only a canary for comfort and company. Utterly Victorian, both old ladies wore permanent mourning, and so inseparable were they from their black bombazine dresses that I was convinced they slept in them. Certainly, the idea of any such near-nakedness as my grandmothers in night-dresses was unthinkable.

Visits to my grandmothers were a daily event, but the high point of the week was the great muster of aunts, uncles and cousins

—first and second—for the noisy ritual of Sunday lunch, the big tea and a gathering afterwards around the piano. At the time, it was all pure bliss although, in retrospect, the piano playing and singing, the duets and solos were probably pretty ghastly. But the eyes and mind of the young are mercifully uncritical, for all experiences are new, and thus to be enjoyed to the utmost.

My sister Florence, who had a good, strong contralto voice, was greatly in demand on these occasions, but the star turn was her fiancé, who had a wavery baritone that could set many a heart trembling. I can still picture him leaning against the piano running through his repertoire, which always reached a climax with a very torrid rendering of a song, 'Thora, speak to me, Thor-a', which was also the signal for a rush to the beer and home-made lemonade.

By far the most dramatic memory of my very early life was the clamour in our road that greeted the declaration of the First World War. It may seem incredible in these days, when people are so sickened and weary of war and violence, that this declaration should have produced such excitement and delight, but people did actually dance in the streets. I was there, and I saw them, and I have never forgotten the scene.

Like most small boys, I delighted in the thrills of war. Nothing that has happened in my life since can quite equal the thrill of the dash for the safety of the broom cupboard under the stairs after the local policeman had pedalled furiously up Lyndhurst Road on his bicycle, blowing his whistle and shouting that enemy Zeppelins were approaching. Neither can I really match the day that my father carried me out into the road to watch a Zeppelin being engaged and actually shot down over Potters Bar, like a huge cigar flaring through the summer sky.

A year after the declaration of war, there was a special celebration at my home when my sister's fiancé returned from France on leave, displaying the Military Medal. To mark the occasion, he brought me a present of a box of fireworks. Unable to resist temptation, I struck a match to light a Roman candle, but forgot

11

to remove the fireworks from the box—or didn't realise that I should. The entire collection went up in an almighty, unscheduled display. This still ranks as one of the major disasters of my boyhood! Perhaps this accounts for my passion for fireworks in later years, which Dee always found amusing—but more of that later! Sadly, a few months later, Florence's fiancé was posted 'missing—believed killed.'

I was eight when the war ended, and the armistice coincided with another great event in my life—I was accepted for the choir of St Michael's, our parish church, and came under the influence of the vicar, the Reverend Midwinter.

I had been enrolled in the local church school at the age of five, and so Mr Midwinter seemed to me to be a giant of a man. He was one of the old school of clergymen who ruled his parish with a kind of benevolent autocracy. But in addition to his manner, he had a great knowledge and love of music, and so to be selected for the choir was regarded as a considerable social caché.

For the next five years the choir and the church became the centre of my life. Today that may sound rather dull, because we have become conditioned to mechanical amusements, paying to be entertained, watching other people play games rather than playing games ourselves, or watching TV, that window on a world of make-believe that so many confuse with reality. Then, the fun was taking part in things; life was generally infinitely more simple and, knowing nothing of the world outside Wood Green, I was perfectly content.

All three schools that I attended were grouped round the church —Infants behind the church, Intermediate beside the church hall, and the Secondary just across the road. On Monday evenings, we went to the church hall for boxing and gymnastics, and on Tuesday evenings there were Cub and Boy Scouts meetings in the church hall. Choir practice was on Wednesday and Friday, and twice on Sunday, at morning and evening services, I took my place in the choir stalls.

The great event of the year was a production of a Gilbert and Sullivan opera by the local operatic society. Our choir was always called on to help pad out the chorus, and so at the age of ten I found myself facing my first audience as a love-sick maiden of *Patience*. We didn't take our roles too seriously and I particularly remember the point where the lead soprano tragically cries: 'Love feeds on hope, they say, or love will die', to which we cheerfully warbled: 'Ah! Misery'. Later on in life I proved just how true these words were.

Some time during my stretch at St Michael's, a misguided public-spirited person decided that a junior concert party could perform a worthwhile civic service. We were called The Redcaps, though any resemblance between us and the Military Police could only have been a figment of a wildly disturbed imagination. Our uniform consisted of Harlequin diamond tops and bottoms and—wait for it!—decorative red caps.

We ranged, with our concerts, over a wide area. Our venues—church halls; our audiences—the very young and the very old. The old were our best audiences, because most of them were chair-bound, and those that were not had to wait for the same buses that transported the maimed, the halt and the blind. Never was there such a captive audience. They just had to sit it out!

Two years after my début in the chorus I was picked to play Ruth, the pirate maid-of-all-work in *The Pirates of Penzance*. An ill-fitting dress, and an extremely tatty wig, with lots of talcum-powder, transformed me, at the age of twelve, into one of the oldest women in Gilbert and Sullivan.

Great friends of my family at this time were some people named Sutters, whose son was a chorister at All Saints', Margaret Street, a contemporary there of Laurence Olivier. They also had a daughter who was a pupil of the famous teacher and agent of child actors, dancers and other such monsters, Italia Conti. I cannot exactly recall how I became involved, but I think Mrs Sutters suggested that it would keep me out of mischief, and earn me a little pocket money over the Christmas holidays, if I went to see Miss Conti.

Every year at Christmas time, this redoubtable lady produced

13

two plays for children: *Where the Rainbow Ends*, a madly flag-waving piece, in which she used anthills of children as fairies, elves, frogs and waterlilies; and *The Windmill Man*, whose cast we believed was made up of roughs who, we felt, with the arrogance of childhood, were less talented than we were. On reflection, therefore, one did not HAVE to be a child prodigy in order to become one of Miss Conti's pupils!

I found the idea of acting during the holidays not unacceptable. Miss Conti was approached, and in due course I was summoned to her offices in Great Ormond Street, opposite the Hospital for Sick Children. There I was confronted by that extraordinary triumvirate—Italia, Bianca and Evelyn Martheze. Only later, of course, was I to become aware of the particular niche in the organisation occupied by the three women—Italia, the dancer and elocutionist with a splendid contralto voice, and so magnificently poised; Bianca, the character actress, the most approachable of the three; the withdrawn, gimlet-eyed Evelyn, the office martinet.

After a few questions, during which I am sure they had become aware of my middle-class accent, Italia suddenly boomed, 'Repeat after me: HOW NOW, BROWN COW?'

Fortunately I have a fair talent for mimicry, and my version received a nod of approval. 'Now say, Round the rugged rocks the ragged rascal ran.' This test, too, I passed with flying colours.

Mrs Sutters, who knew the Misses Conti, of course, had come with me. She was handed a contract for my parents to sign. I was to receive thirty shillings for six performances a week, and there were agency and tuition options for the next five years. I was to understudy the juvenile lead, play the Elf King, etc. I was to be given two and sixpence for pocket-money, five shillings for fares, and the balance would be put in a Post Office account by the Conti office.

And that is how it started, in all seriousness. I adored it from the first moment. The excitement, the thrill, the smell of the theatre went right down to one's toes. Indeed, it had to, if one were to stay the course.

14

There was a great deal of music in *The Rainbow*, written by that gentle, talented and so English composer, Roger Quilter. At rehearsals in the old Holborn Empire, Italia would plant herself in front of the orchestra pit, and, at the top of her voice, sing out the dance steps to the melodies of the ballet music. I can still hear her singing. 'Jeté, jeté, coupé—*up*! Jeté, jeté, coupé—*up*! Into the middle and hands up—oh!'

At the time, no one thought it funny or odd, but looking back and remembering contorts me with silent laughter.

Surely there was no transformation to equal that Christmas, my elevation from Wood Green church hall to the stage of one of London's most famous theatres, the Holborn Empire, one of the loveliest of the old music halls, with its gilded plaster and red plush! It certainly made my Christmas an 'over the rainbow' one.

Miss Conti's 'children' played only matinées. As soon as we had stored away our bits of grease-paint in old cigar boxes or soap boxes, and taken our costumes to the wardrobe, the dressing-rooms were taken over by the mighty ones of the music hall, for their 'twice nightly' performances. George Robey, Little Tich, Ernie Mayne, Nellie Wallace, Hetty King—I saw them all, and by God, were they good!

The four-week season ended all too soon, and it was back to school and the choir stalls. The glory was over; that was that. The end of an era; the close of a life!

Even though the past few weeks soon seemed little more than a Christmas fantasy, I had tasted the real thing. I had known the thrill of a full house, the brightness of the limelights, and after such delights, amateur operatics and singing in the choir seemed very dull fare.

Weeks passed and, for the first time, I experienced the feeling with which I was to become so familiar, and to which all actors are accustomed; I would never act again. Then quite unexpectedly a telegram arrived for me from Italia Conti. This simply said: 'Please attend New Theatre tomorrow 2.30'. Nowadays, of course, mother would have telephoned the Contis to ask what this request meant, but, as I have said, life was simpler then; we had no telephone in our house, and it never crossed our mind to use the public 'phone in the local post office. In our reasoning, there must be an important reason for sending a telegram, and it never occurred to either of us to query the summons.

Fortunately, the next day was Wednesday, and in the afternoon we had our weekly 'sport recreational session'. No one would miss me from that so, accompanied by my mother, I caught a No 29 bus to take me to the West End. In those days, the fare from Wood Green to Trafalgar Square was 4d; now it is 15p.

Italia was waiting for us at the stage door of the New Theatre. We went into a gloomy passage backstage, where she explained that I was to audition for the part of the page-boy in a new play by George Bernard Shaw called *St Joan*. I barely had time to take in all this, or even to think whether this was what I wanted, before we were summoned to a dressing-room where Sybil Thorndike, who was to create the part of St Joan, and her husband, Lewis Casson, were waiting. I was aware of another person in the room, apparently perched on the mantelpiece, dressed in very hairy tweeds, and with a mass of red hair on his face and head.

Lewis Casson handed me a few pages of typescript and told me to read the part of Dunois' page with him. I had hardly got to the end of the first line, when George Bernard Shaw, for that was who he was, clambered down from his precarious seat, and snatched the papers from me with a ferocious cry of: 'No, boy! Like THIS', and in a ridiculous falsetto read: 'Look, look! There she goes'. I thought he was quite mad, but nevertheless tried to mimic him.

A few minutes more and it was all over, and my mother and I were out in the street again, waiting for a bus to take us home. I don't think that either of us thought that the audition had gone very well and when, after some days, we heard nothing, we were quite sure I had not got the part. But then another peremptory telegram arrived from Italia Conti. This time it read: 'Please attend at my office this evening after five with your father'. Since

16

I was under-age my father had to sign all my contracts, and so, after all, it was clear that I had the part.

I suspect that my parents thought it extremely odd that their youngest son should have been picked out to perform in a major London production, but whatever doubts they might have had, they never voiced them to me. They never lavished anything but encouragement on me, and for this I have always been grateful.

Neither of them ever showed any theatrical leanings, but they both shared a great love of the theatre, and one luxury they allowed themselves was regular Friday night seats in the front row of the circle at the Wood Green Empire; and whether there was variety or drama on the bill, they were always there. This was as sacred a ritual as Sunday church-going.

I have often wondered what thoughts went through my father's mind as he sat in Italia Conti's office filling out my application form for a London County Council juvenile's work permit, and carefully signing the contract that bound me to the Thorndikes. But I don't think that either of us realised that, as he signed, he was signing me off from Wood Green for ever. One chapter of my life had ended, another was about to begin.

During my Christmas shows my attendance at school was very infrequent; so much so that, on joining my class one day, the headmaster peered over his spectacles and remarked drily: 'Ah, Hawkins, paying us one of your fleeting visits?'

Now other arrangements were being made for my future education, and on the morning I arrived at the New Theatre to start my acting career in earnest I met someone who was to have a lasting impact on my life. She was Miss Maisie East, a small, round, incredibly energetic woman who had been appointed as my companion, guardian and teacher. I was immediately struck by her incredibly bright, inquiring eyes. Nothing seemed to escape her attention, which was just as well for me, for there were some considerable homosexuals in the cast.

But her role was more than merely that of protector of my virtue and morals. She helped me with my career and nurtured

17

and moulded it with extraordinary care and skill, as enthusiastic-ally as if it were her own. She also guided me into the part of Dunois' page, taught me the lore of the theatre, and how to accept the extremely rigid discipline which was imposed on actors in those days. And at the same time she gave me an educa-tion which was far superior to anything I could have hoped to receive in a secondary school in the early 1920s. As a teacher, she was far ahead of her time. She realised that we can learn from every experience, and when I was not actually working in the theatre, she would take me away on trips.

One experience I will always remember involved going with the production of *St Joan* to the Théâtre des Champs Elysées in Paris. We flew from Croydon in a rather frail Hercules, which was an experience in itself. Twenty-stone Bruce Winston, in charge of the wardrobe, was so enraptured by the experience that he paced up and down the tiny cabin, until the captain, who had to keep turning the aircraft, because of the shifting weight, ordered him to his seat.

In Paris, we climbed every church tower from Notre Dame downwards, with the Eiffel Tower thrown in for good measure. Not a museum or art gallery missed our attention. We explored Versailles and picnicked in the Fontainebleau Forest. And after this week of furious academic exertion, we spent golden days on the Normandy coast.

Even when we were on tour with a play, she found time or rather, made time, for more museums and galleries and educa-tional visits to factories. In Scotland, for example, we boated on Loch Lomond, clambered up to Arthur's Seat in Edinburgh, rambled in the Highlands. In Bath and Chester, we studied the Roman ruins.

But all the time my real education was taking place in the theatre, where I was being taught my craft as an actor by a remark-able, if sometimes eccentric, team of teachers. Above all, I was taught to love and respect words. Each word had to be the right word; and each had to be spoken in a way that its weight and importance demanded. In the early 1920s, long before method acting was heard of, the delivery and use of words was still the most important aspect of acting, and here I had a superb master in Lewis Casson, who loved to 'tune' the scripted word.

He had such a passion for language that any slip-shod delivery would bring down a flood of Welsh fury on the head of the wretched actor. Basil Dean, who was later to have a profound effect on my career, was another fanatical devotee of intonation and inflection; and John Gielgud never failed to mesmerise me with his extraordinary command of poetry. But none of them equalled Harley Granville Barker's superb understanding of the Shakespearean canon.

I was once rehearsing *King Lear*, in which I was playing Edmund under his direction. He silenced me in mid-soliloquy, and asked the prompter: 'Isn't there a comma in the middle of that last sentence?'

The prompter studied the script.

'Yes, Mr Barker,' he agreed.

'Mr Hawkins,' said HGB sternly, 'observe it!'

But, to return . . .

The *St Joan* company was rich in characters, and one I grew most fond of was Bruce Winston, who acted, as well as being in charge of making the costumes which were designed by Charles Rickets. I first met Bruce in the wardrobe department at the New Theatre. Surrounded by bales of velvet, moire silk and damask, he looked exactly like a medieval cloth merchant.

Most of us lived in fear of Thomas Warren, the stage manager, who demanded and received absolute obedience. But in spite of his austere and autocratic manner, he rescued me from a disaster which still brings me out in a sweat when I recall it.

This happened during the dress rehearsal for the first performance of *St Joan*. There is a scene where Dunois and the Maid meet, and I was perched on a hillock guarding Dunois' great shield and lance. At the end of the scene, when Dunois and Joan were leaving the stage, I had to tug the lance from the ground, pick up the shield, and jump down to the rostrum, and from there down

19

three steps to stage level, shouting: 'The Maid, the Maid! God and the Maid! Hurray-ay-ay!'

Then, according to the stage directions, I was to 'caper out after them, mad with excitement'. I followed these directions faultlessly, but by the time I hit the stage level I had lost control of the heavy lance. The point swung forward and plunged through the extremely beautiful stage-drop which was then coming down. There was a horrified silence, and I was close to tears when I saw the damage I had done. Tommy Warren stalked across the stage and without saying a word carefully extracted the lance from the rent in the drop. Then he turned to me. I expected a frightful blasting, possibly even dismissal, but he simply said: 'Don't worry, boy. It's not your fault. We should have tested this out long before now.'

I have always remembered how lightly he let me off, and several times since then, when someone with whom I have been working has made some idiotic mistake, and I have been tempted to bawl them out, I have heard Tommy Warren's quiet voice in my mind, and swallowed my annoyance.

Raymond Massey was also in the cast, playing Captain La Hire. He and various others ran a book on the date my voice would break, because then I would have to leave. Ironically, in view of later events, my voice never broke, but gradually grew deeper. When it did break in 1966, it broke for ever—and Ray was there to hear it. But that time, he had no bet on it.

By the end of my first year with the Casson–Thorndike company, I was not only playing Dunois' page in the evenings, but also taking the part of Crispian in *Where the Rainbow Ends* at matinees. Altogether I stayed with the company for three years.

I was appointed assistant-assistant stage manager, I touched up scenery, and played an endless succession of roles, because, apart from *St Joan*, we staged productions of Shakespeare's *Henry VIII*, *Medea* and Shelley's *The Cenci*. It was in this last play that I earned one of the best reviews of my life, when the great critic of the day, James Agate, wrote in *The Sunday Times*: 'It is possible that in Master Jack Hawkins we have a very fine actor in the making. I have certainly never seen a boy-player of so much promise.'

But I was not the only boy actor in the company. Two of my companions were Laurence Olivier and Carol Reed.

On one of our tours I remember a crazy exotic frolic of Carol's. I think we were in Liverpool and in a street market he suddenly spotted a caged fox for sale. This was more than he could bear, and he bought it and took it back to his digs. It was all very laudable, but a little tricky, to say the least. He let it loose with some water and some mince, locked his room and went to the theatre.

On his return he was met by a furious landlady complaining of the smell on the landing. He made some excuse, and went to his room. To his dismay there was no sign of the wretched animal, but presently he heard some faint scratches coming from on high, and there was reynard perched on top of the wardrobe. From his description, I would not recommend teetering on a rickety bed-room chair, trying to prise a wild fox off the top of a wardrobe. With some difficulty he managed it, however, got it back to its cage and set it free in the country next morning. I have a feeling that this idiotic anecdote may be a pointer to Carol's marvellously gentle approach to the actors he now directs in films!

Years later, our paths crossed again. Carol directed *Fallen Idol*, the second film I made when I came out of the Army after the war—which was also the first I made after my marriage to Dee.

In 1926, the company was very nearly ruined by the General Strike. The strike coincided with the opening of a new London season of *St Joan*, but because of street demonstrations and the fact that buses and tubes were not running, few people were prepared to go to the theatre. In those days, of course, relatively few people owned cars and many of those who did were reluctant to drive in London.

Determined to arrive at rehearsals on time, I set off at six in the morning to walk the eight miles from Wood Green to the New— but unfortunately arrived five minutes late.

I apologised but did not explain why. However, someone

mentioned the real reason to the Cassons and from then on they very generously insisted I stay with them. In fact, I became like one of their family and, to this day, she always refers to me as 'little Jack'!

It was typical of the Cassons' belief in Socialism that while every evening the play was being slaughtered financially by the strike, every following morning Lewis would drive TUC leaders to their meetings with Government ministers in his blue Lanchester. In those days, trades union leaders could not afford their own cars.

Each evening, we would go through the ritual of a performance for the handful of people who formed the audience. Before the curtain went up, either Lewis or the stage manager would go out in front and invite them to come down to the front row of the stalls.

'We shall feel more cosy,' he would explain. But, eventually, the situation grew so bad that we were forced to close.

There were some ugly incidents at that time. Opposite the Lyceum was the *Morning Post* building. This paper's presses were being used to produce the *British Gazette*, the official Government newsheet, which Winston Churchill edited. Volunteer students off-loaded the newsprint to jeers and jostling from the strikers.

One afternoon, as I was going to visit Hamley's wonderful toy-shop, or the model railway experts, Bassett-Lowke's, down High Holborn came tanks and lorries full of helmeted soldiers. Rumours rushed round; they were coming from the docks with food; they were going to the docks to get the food; no one knew the truth of it. But there it was—the Army in central London!

The last time I had been conscious of that was, of course, the First World War, when local contingents used to march around, generally in civilian clothes still, wearing an arm-band or some such lethal weapon. My father was one, and that is why I remember, I suppose. I was five at the time and very proud of him. My pride was to be short-lived, however, for he was found medically unfit. The doctors decided that he had a very bad patch of TB on a lung. He died a few years ago, aged eighty-six!

By the end of the year, when the strike was over and life was beginning to return to normal, I was made assistant-assistant stage manager for a production of *Macbeth*, in which I played the part of Banquo's son, Fleance.

For some reason, George Bernard Shaw decided to attend rehearsals and 'help' Lewis Casson with the production. He lost little time in putting everyone's backs up with his comments and his way of uttering them. Lewis managed to keep the peace, until one day when the final lines of the play—

> 'So thanks to all at once, and to each one
> Whom we invite to see us crowned at Scone'—

were being spoken. No sooner had the last word been said than GBS pranced down to the orchestra rails, and in his Irish voice declared:

'No! no! It should be pronounced SKOON!'

This was too much for the Scottish actor John Laurie, now so well known for his TV appearances in *Dad's Army*. He was playing Lennox, and he strode to the footlights, and in his splendid rolling voice, said: 'Mr Shaw, you are talking rubbish. I am Scots born and bred. The place is called SKON. It always has been SKON, and no Irishman is going to change it!'

One cloud that hung over the production was the health of Henry Ainley, the Shakespearean actor who was playing Macbeth. He was suffering from a mental collapse and drinking heavily. A combination of troubles began to affect his voice. I suppose that man for man I have never seen such a combination of beauty in looks and voice since Henry Ainley. I appeared briefly in about three scenes, so most of the time I spent in the prompt corner. But when Ainley started to crack, he did not take kindly to the call-boy. For no reason we could discover, he would wander off into dark recesses of the stage, mumbling to himself, mainly his lines for the next scene and then so often miss his entrance cue. To overcome this, it was decided that I should be his 'shepherd'.

We got along very well together. I worshipped him and I think he realised I was just there to help. I would go up to his dressing room about five minutes before he was due on stage, and he would

23

greet me with, 'My dea-ar boy!' and I would reply, 'Ready, sir?'
'I think so. Let us go down.'

Going along the corridor, there would inevitably be the regal inquiry, 'Well, what have we been doing today?'

'Sir, I had ballet class this morning, and fencing class this afternoon.'

'Splendid! Splendid! Keep working, keep doing everything!'

Just before we reached stage level, he would start testing his voice, with a series of 'Mmmmmm's and 'Me-me-me's, and I would open the doors and we would pass through. I kept very close to him, and, when his cue came, moved aside and on he went.

One evening as we went through the regular ritual, 'My dea-ar boy etc.', I noticed that his voice had an unpleasant rasp. He was fairly silent going down to the stage, and when he went on stage, his opening lines were very forced. By the end of the performance his voice had gone completely. It was a shattering experience to see and hear his agony. He was only forty-seven, and it would be three long years before he reappeared in the theatre.

How little then did I realise what this loss of voice must have meant to him—or what it would mean to me.

The end of my time with Lewis and Sybil's company marked the beginning of perhaps the worst patch in all my acting career.

I was asked to audition for a part in a play called *Interference*, which was playing at the St James's Theatre with a cast headed by Sir Gerald du Maurier and Frank Lawton. The plan was to set up a touring company to take the play to the provinces while the London cast stayed at the St James's. I was given the main juvenile part and a contract for a summer season in the south coast resorts—Brighton, Folkestone, Bognor and Southsea. If it went well, there would be another tour in the New Year.

Naturally, I was delighted, but we had not been on the road long before I became the whipping boy of the stage manager and his wife. The stage manager was also playing the part of a police-man, and his wife was assistant-stage manager, and an understudy. This was a very cosy arrangement for them, but not, as I was to discover, as cosy as it could have been for me. They had banked

24

on their son playing my part, but unfortunately I had beaten him at the auditions. They always reminded me of Mr and Mrs Squeers in *Nicholas Nickleby*, with me in the unfortunate role of the wretched Smike. When anything went wrong, Hawkins was to blame. If the theatre cat wandered on to the stage, I was responsible. If someone slammed the door, that was my fault. If the property man forgot to fill the cigarette box for a scene, this was because I had been talking to him.

Because I was so conditioned by the discipline of the theatre, I never answered back, which on reflection was foolish, but when the management visited us at Weston-super-Mare and said they wished us all to stay on for a winter season, I claimed that I had family problems, and left.

Back in London, I called on Italia Conti, expecting her to be furious, but instead she said I could play the lead part of St George in *Where the Rainbow Ends*.

This was a marvellous part—my first stage hero. The only problem was that I had to wear a suit of armour which seemed to weigh at least a ton. Quite my best moment was when I made my entrance disguised as an ancient monk after my summons by the Genii of the Carpet. I would stand on the stage draped in my monk's habit, while a property man reached up through a tiny trap-door and gathered a knot of cords hanging down the back and pulled them, while a magnesium flash was ignited by the footlights. When the smoke cleared, I would be in a blazing floodlight, clad in shining armour from head to foot.

However, this was a brief moment of glory, and when the Christmas season ended, I was completely out of work. Sitting at home in Wood Green was intolerable, and so every day I took a bus to the West End, and wandered round the theatres, gazing at the stage doors that were now closed to me.

One day I was walking gloomily down St Martin's Lane, and had stopped outside the New Theatre to look at the bills and photographs of the current production, when the main doors opened and Bronson Albery, who controlled the New, Wyndhams and Criterion theatres, came down the steps. I knew him quite well from the *St Joan* days, and he greeted me and asked what I was doing.

'Nothing,' I replied. 'Just looking at theatres.'

'I was thinking about you the other day,' he said. 'Basil Dean is looking for some good young actors for a new play, and I mentioned your name, but nobody seemed to know where you were. Give him a ring. Say I told you to.'

I ran down to St Martin's Court, where I knew there was a telephone box, found Basil Dean's number in the directory, and dialled it. When I got through and gave my name the response was about as exciting as last week's suet pudding. But when I mentioned that Bronson Albery had asked me to ring, the atmosphere thawed a little, and I was told to be at their office in John Street, Adelphi, at three o'clock.

It was then only about one o'clock, and the following two hours were the longest I had ever spent. I went to the National Gallery; killed a little time at Lyons, eating a poached egg on toast; and finally took the longest and most circuitous route possible to John Street. Even then I managed to arrive five minutes early.

Oddly enough, this first visit to the National Gallery before an important appointment was the beginning of a pattern that I have repeated many times since then on the eve of big decisions and first nights.

I introduced myself to Miss Hamilton, the secretary, who lived in a tiny glass cubicle. She handed me an envelope.

'Come with me,' she said. 'Mr Dean will see you now.'

We stopped at a door at the end of a long passage, knocked, and a thin, precise voice said: 'Come in.'

Basil Dean peered at me through pebble-lenses from behind a desk. He saw the envelope in my hand.

'I see you have your part,' he said approvingly. 'We start rehearsals in ten days' time.'

That was the end of the interview. I paced up and down the Strand for ten minutes before summoning the courage to return to the office. Miss Hamilton was back in her glass cage when I returned.

'What exactly is all this about?' I asked.

'Don't you know?' she asked, surprised. 'It's a play by John van Druten called *Young Woodley*. It has been refused a licence by the Lord Chamberlain. It's going to be produced at the 300 Club on a Sunday evening, and then go to a private theatre club, The Arts, for two weeks.'

# THREE

*Young Woodley* marked a crucial turning point in my career. It confirmed the fact that I was no longer a boy actor, but was now accepted for juvenile roles, and so at last on the road that led to adult parts. This was important because the theatre has an unpleasant habit of not allowing child actors to grow up.

Admittedly, I was only just over seventeen, and had been cast as the school prefect, Ainger, in the play, but it was an extremely adult play dealing with passionate adult emotions. To combine passion with an English public school setting, between a boy and a master's wife, at that time was more than the Lord Chamberlain could tolerate, and this was why he withheld his licence. Added to this was the fact that I was to be directed by Basil Dean, one of the greatest directors in the British theatre, and I felt every right to be walking on air. And by what a stroke of luck or chance had the part become mine! Had I not taken a walk down St Martin's Lane . . .

By the time the first day of rehearsals arrived I was in a state of extreme agitation, and arrived at the theatre half an hour ahead of time, only to find the other junior members of the cast— Henry Mollison, Derek de Marney and Frank Lawton—already there.

We were all pretty agitated, having heard some hair-raising stories of Basil Dean's sarcasm and intolerance of sloppy acting. There was one particular legend of a leading man who was so cruelly flayed by BD's tongue that he fainted on the stage. At this, Basil slipped on his coat, glanced at the unconscious actor, and said: 'I think we will break for lunch.'

When he arrived at the old Playhouse Theatre where we were rehearsing he gave us all a curt good morning and said that, providing we acted the play as he wanted it acted, he had no doubt that the Lord Chamberlain would lift the ban.

Needless to say, I caught the edge of his tongue during the gruelling rehearsals. In one scene, I had to make an entrance through a window to visit Young Woodley, who had been expelled for kissing his housemaster's wife. I made my entrance, only to be stopped short by the familiar icy voice from the back of the theatre.

'Where's the knife, Hawkins?'

I was panic-stricken. I couldn't remember anything about a knife in the script.

'What knife, sir?' I stammered.

'From the way you appeared in the window, I was convinced you were going to kill him,' he retorted.

At dress rehearsals, it is always the director's habit, after each act, to hand notes to those of the cast he considered were giving what he called 'a performance'. After the first act of the dress rehearsal for Young Woodley Basil Dean marched over to the youngest actor, a small boy playing Cope, the fag and prefect's general dogsbody.

'Very good,' he said, 'but have some more inkstains put on your collar.'

Turning to us, he snapped: 'As for the rest of you, it was bloody awful. Reset the stage. We will start from the beginning again.'

This may not seem unreasonable, but the average dress rehearsal, with lighting and scene changes, can last for twelve hours. You can imagine our feelings at having to start all over again at midnight.

None of us knew what was 'bloody awful', and years later, when I was on much closer terms with Basil, I reminded him of the incident, and asked what was wrong with our performances. At first he pretended not to recall the occasion. Then he said: 'You were all so cocky and acting with such confidence, you could not have been less like schoolboys. I had to take you down a peg or two.' And, of course, he succeeded.

In spite of his sharpness, Basil was basically a kind and generous man. Once the Lord Chamberlain's ban was lifted on the play, which happened within a short time, it settled down to a huge success, and we were all summoned to Basil's office to discuss our salaries. I had never earned more than £5 a week, and had great hopes of having this increased to £8, a very considerable income then, at a time when the average wage for the country was £2.10s. a week. With studied vagueness Dean asked me: 'What part do you play?'

'Ainger, sir,' I told him.

'Ah, yes, of course. I pay £10 a week for that part.'

This was an unbelievably princely sum for a young actor in those days. A short time afterwards, I was put on a three-year contract at £10 a week for the current year, £20 for the second and £30 for the third. With such unexpected riches at my command I went out and bought my first car—a beautiful plum-coloured Fiat, with fawn upholstery, buttoned seats, and cut-glass flower vases inside on the door pillars. It cost me £60. Since then, I have owned Bentleys and Jaguars, but no other car has ever given me quite the same degree of pleasure as that first little Fiat.

This car was the cause of my being rushed to hospital with double pneumonia. I was so proud that I spent all one Sunday morning cleaning it in the hot July sun and then took my mother for what we called 'a spin' in the country. On the return journey I felt increasingly ill with a blinding pain in my head and indeed only just managed to get the car into our driveway before I blacked out.

Forty years later, I had almost exactly the same experience. I was on holiday with Dee and Peter and Sian O'Toole in Mexico when again I had this fearful pain. The doctors shrugged it off by assuring me it was only 'Montezuma's Curse'. I was determined not to spoil the holiday for the others and so made light of it. But back in New York I saw another doctor who made a different diagnosis: I had been walking about for ten days with double pneumonia. The treatment nowadays with modern antibiotics is happily quicker, more effective and less humiliating than being subjected to the late 1920s treatment of constant hot poultices in the small of my back. As they cooled, they crumbled, so that I felt as though I were sleeping in a bed filled with old bread crusts. Happier memories of this illness are of a steady supply of medicinal brandy.

Basil Dean demonstrated his kindness by sending me on a return trip to the Canary Islands by banana boat, to recuperate. Without wishing to detract from his generosity, I am bound to admit I have been on more agreeable cruises—and it put me off bananas for a very long time!

When I returned to the cast of *Young Woodley* Basil Dean told me that he wanted me to play opposite Laurence Olivier in a huge, spectacular production of *Beau Geste*. He was to play Beau, and I would be his younger brother, John. *Beau Geste* was disaster-ridden from the start, but at least it was a spectacular disaster, and surprisingly one that was fun to be involved with.

With his usual obsession for detail and authenticity, Basil Dean was quite determined that we would all be expert French Foreign Legionnaires by the first night. At nine o'clock every morning during rehearsals we had to turn up at an extremely smelly little gymnasium in Villiers Street, just off the Strand, for a punishing work-out. From there, we would rush to His Majesty's Theatre, where a Regimental Sgt-Major from one of the Guards Regiments was waiting to give us three-quarters of an hour of square-bashing, and only after this did we start the acting rehearsals. We finished each day with an hour's singing of soldiers' choruses and marching songs, written by Ernest Irving, who was later to write most of the background music for Ealing Studios' films.

Sometimes, the going was pretty rough. One day, when we were doing a semi-dress rehearsal for a fight scene in the barracks, I was knocked out cold when someone kicked me on the head with the hefty studded Army boots that Basil insisted we wore. Everything was to be authentic down to the last button and bullet. BD bought a job lot of very insanitary Foreign Legion uniforms from the French Government, so authentic that even repeated fumigation could not make them pleasant to wear.

31

In one scene, I had to fire a Maxim gun from a turret in the desert fort. Unfortunately, the blanks we were using failed to activate the gun's automatic firing mechanism, so soft wood bullets were inserted in the cartridges. These worked wonderfully. With my first burst I cut three feet off the bottom of the cyclorama cloth that ran round the stage. From then on, I had to fire on a low trajectory, and showers of splinters exploded from the stage as the bullets struck. It was a miracle that nobody was injured, and the battle scene was so realistic on the first night that two women fainted in the front row, and quite a number of the audience dived for cover.

The opening night was a shambles, particularly the final scene. In this Beau is dead, and so is a vile character, a sergeant, and lots of others, good and bad. In fact, I think I was the only character left 'alive'. Beau had always wanted a Viking funeral, so I had to heave Larry Olivier on to a bed, drape him with the flag, and dump the sergeant at his feet. I then had to pour petrol over the corpses—in fact, on some sand by the side of their bodies—and put a match to the funeral pyre. Smoke instantly began to fill the stage, and a cunningly contrived sheet of silk was flashed up to simulate flames.

It so happened that the theatre fireman on duty was new to his job and had not seen the dress rehearsals. He therefore imagined that the theatre was ablaze and about to burn down. With real gallantry, he hurled himself into the prompt corner and pulled the emergency release for the fire curtain, a vast contraption of iron and asbestos, which immediately crashed down on to the stage.

The audience apparently went wild with excitement, but this was lost on us because the handles used to raise the fire curtain manually had been mislaid. By the time they were found, the curtain raised, and we were assembled to take our bows, the theatre was empty. It was therefore no surprise to any of us involved that we were not set for a long run. *Beau Geste* folded after eight weeks.

Fortunately for me, during the last week of the horrific run of

*Beau Geste*, James Welch, the director of *Journey's End*, which was having an enormous success in the West End, asked me to audition for the leading part—Stanhope—for the New York production. I did so, was offered the part with leave of absence from Basil Dean, a contract for two hundred dollars a week, and a first-class return passage to New York. Two hundred dollars was the equivalent of £40, and in those days—1929—a pound in your pocket really was worth a pound. My salary, in today's terms, would probably be worth £200 a week—and I was still only eighteen.

This seemed to be the big break for which some actors wait until they are old, and some never find at all. The part had already made a star of Colin Clive in London, and now I was sure that it would do the same for me. But then chance, fate, call it what you will, stepped in.

During a coffee-break in rehearsals shortly after we had started working on the play, one of the actors said he hoped he could get away early because it was his birthday and he wanted to take his wife out to lunch. The conversation turned to age generally, and someone turned to me and asked how old I was.

'Eighteen,' I replied without thinking.

When we broke for lunch, Gilbert Miller, the New York theatre owner who had bought the American rights of the play, invited me to join him at the Savoy. I was agreeably flattered. Lunch at the Savoy was clearly something to which I was going to have to grow accustomed. I found it no hardship. Jimmy Welch joined us in the American Bar.

'Tell me, Jack, you're not REALLY only eighteen, are you?' Gilbert asked, after we had ordered drinks.

'Yes, and a bit,' I assured him. I was proud of what I had achieved at an age when many of my contemporaries were still at school.

There was an uncomfortable pause while we waited for the drinks to arrive. Then Gilbert's distinctive high-pitched, nasal twang broke the silence.

'Look, Jack, this is a very important production,' he said. 'I'm

33

putting it on at one of the theatres I control in New York—the Henry Miller. I shall have to transfer a show that is already there, so you see a lot of money is at stake, and I just don't feel it can rest on the shoulders of a guy of eighteen.'

My dreams of stardom took a sudden swift nose-dive, but Jimmy stepped in to my rescue. He said that he wanted me in the company to understudy Stanhope, and before I could refuse this apparent humiliation, he added that he was not happy with the actor who played Lieutenant Hibbert, the coward, and wanted me to replace him.

In the end, Jimmy took over the lead himself, as well as directing, and I would be second lead, with my contract unchanged. In fact, Jimmy later relinquished the part of Stanhope, and gave it to another actor, Colin Keith-Johnston. But all in all this was a fine piece of diplomacy, and I appreciated it. It also taught me never to count on anything happening—until it had happened. As someone said, blessed is he who expects nothing, for he is never disappointed. This is a very sound motto for any actor to follow, and one which, over the years, I have always found full of wisdom, if not of comfort!

I did have one satisfying moment of revenge. Just before we were due to sail for New York, we did six public performances of the American production at the Arts Theatre Club. Most of the critics gave pretty savage reviews—'What will America think of our famous war play? New York unlikely to see the play at its best'—was the general tone. But E. A. Baugham, of the *Daily News*, wrote: 'Jack Hawkins, who plays the part of Lt. Hibbert, would make a better Captain Stanhope,' which was a nice bit of nose-thumbing at Gilbert Miller.

The trip to America aboard the *Aquitania* was one long party. In 1929, America was in the grip of prohibition, and, faced with a long dry spell, we regarded it as our duty to take on as much drink as we could while we had the opportunity.

Every day of that five-day journey was a party, ending with a magnificent deluge of booze on the last night at sea, as we emptied bottle after bottle in recognition of our 'last drink'. We had been regaled on the journey with hair-raising tales of bootleg booze that sent you blind and mad after a couple of nips, so that we really did believe that we were having our last drinkable drinks for as long as the show ran.

Happily this was not so. Colin and I decided to book into the Wentworth Hotel on 46th Street, just off Sixth Avenue, in the middle of New York's theatre area. We both had hangovers when we booked in, and as we were going up to our rooms in the lift, Colin asked the bellhop if he could organise some ginger ale and ice for us.

'Sure. What do you want to go with it?'

'Nothing,' he said hurriedly.

'When you do, let me know. Gin, whisky, anything. It's all good stuff,' the lad assured us.

To be turned loose in New York at the age of eighteen—even though I was very innocent compared with eighteen-year-olds these days—was a most exhilarating experience. For the first time in my life I had money in my pocket, and a career at my feet, and beyond the theatre, no responsibilities. This was the setting for a rake's progress, and one that I was quick to recognise.

After a one-performance shakedown in a small Long Island town called Great Neck, where we played in a cinema with an hoarding outside which declared—'*Journey's End*. A play, not a film. Actors in the FLESH!'—we moved to the Henry Miller theatre to a tremendous reception.

Brooks Atkinson, the leading New York theatre critic at that time, wrote: 'No play in recent years has instantaneously made so profound an impression here as *Journey's End*. Having recently heard (from London) uneasy tidings about the merits of the company, many of us were prepared for disappointment. . . . Not having seen the London production I have no viable standards of comparison. But I can imagine nothing more hauntingly beautiful or affecting than the performance disclosed by our visiting troupe.'

The day after the opening the theatre was booked solid for the next three months.

Apart from this unequivocal success two other things of great importance happened to me in New York. First, I lost my virginity, which I had for some extraordinary reason retained—perhaps through the close guardianship of Miss East, and second I learnt to make bathtub gin.

Sex and drink tend to be addictive and, to some extent, complementary, and since I was by then sharing an enormous flat over the Hudson Theatre on 45th Street, which I leased from Geoffrey Holmesdale, Lord Amherst's heir, I was in need of a ready supply of booze for the parties we held, which were becoming nightly events.

Unless one had the right contacts, getting good liquor was a problem during prohibition. The bootleggers had the ingenious custom of buying bottles of the real stuff, and then draining half of it off through a tiny hole drilled in the bottom of the bottle. They would then top up the bottle with wood alcohol, seal the hole, and sell it as genuine gin.

I tackled a friend of mine who always seemed to have a very ready supply of drinkable gin, and asked him how and where he bought it.

'Nowhere. I make it myself in the bath,' he replied.

What he could do, so could I. He put me in touch with his supplier. All I had to do was dial a Stuyvesant number, give whoever answered a password, and say, 'Jack Hawkins, Henry Miller Theatre. One gallon of White Rose and fixings.'

From the nearest drug store, I bought two gallons of distilled water, and begged as many empty mineral water bottles as I could. I was now ready to set up in business as a distiller. The first time I put in an order I was met at the stage door by a youth carrying a rather obvious brown paper parcel. 'Nineteen dollars', he muttered, and thrust the parcel into my hands. I gave him a twenty-dollar bill, and he scuttled away. The parcel seemed very heavy, and slopped noisily with every step I took. I whistled loudly in an attempt to disguise this tell-tale sound.

First thing the next morning I went into the distilling business. The White Rose was a gallon of pure alcohol, and the 'fixings'

36

were an ounce of glycerin and an ounce of oil of juniper. These I added to the spirit and shook the whole mixture vigorously. So much for the basic ingredients; all that remained was to manufacture the finished product, a simple process of adding one-third of spirit to two-thirds of distilled water in each bottle. Ideally, the gin should then be allowed to 'mature' for a couple of hours, but if the need was pressing it could be drunk immediately. So far as we were concerned, the need was usually pressing.

I don't suppose this will do much for my reputation, but I can honestly record that all my friends who drank Hawkins Gin, and those to whom I taught the art of distilling, are either still alive and well, or have died of natural causes. Certainly, many a happy love affair began and developed over a glass or two of bathtub. Most of my affairs were with English actresses, of whom there were a great number in those days in New York. But there was one exception, a lovely American divorcee, who I met at a cocktail party before an evening performance. Half-way through the show a telegram was delivered to my dressing-room. It read: 'Dear Jack, it was so nice to meet you this evening. I have got a few people coming to my apartment later on. Will you come on after the show.' There was an address, so I thought, why not, and after the curtain call took a taxi to her apartment.

The lovely divorcee ushered me into a totally empty flat. This was an agreeable deception which swiftly developed into a beautifully balanced relationship. Whenever either of us felt lonely we would ring the other, but never was there any sense of obligation.

Whether because I was English, or a successful actor, or maybe a combination of both, I had more than my fair share of lionising. I was 'taken up' by a number of enormously wealthy families who used to invite me to their huge country estates for weekends. One Jewish family I remember very clearly, particularly because they had two beautiful daughters. If I missed seeing them for a week, they would send a chauffeur-driven Cadillac to collect me from the theatre.

They lived in tremendous style about forty miles from New York, with a stable of twenty-five horses, from which I could choose one whenever I wanted. They also had a complex of tennis and squash courts, a swimming pool, and relatives who lived three miles away owned a private nine-hole golf course. I had never imagined life on this scale; it possessed an almost mediaeval grandeur, heightened by the soaring stock market which accentuated the atmosphere of wealth with which we all seemed to be surrounded. And, of course, these revels were even then almost at an end; the stock market crash of 1929 was only weeks away.

On reflection, I think that my happiest hours were spent with the English acting contingent in a Times Square drug store called The Silver Grill. I had to learn a kind of shorthand in order to get anything to eat. 'Burn one' was the call for coffee, and a 'B and T on, hold the grass' meant a bacon and tomato sandwich, toasted, without lettuce. They were good days, and all gilded, looking back, because we were young.

One evening, Emile Littler, who was then stage manager to Arthur Hopkins, sidled over to me and in a whisper said he had some fine brandy in his hotel room, which he would be pleased to share with me. When I arrived at his room, he was displaying the bottle like some kind of rare trophy. He was dressed for the occasion in an artificial silk dressing-gown. The cork proved a little stubborn, and he finally had to grip the bottle between his knees. When the cork finally surrendered, some of the liquid splashed on his knees.

Anyway, we filled our glasses and were about to drink when Emile let out a cry of distress. Where the brandy had slopped on to his dressing-gown were two symmetrical, and quickly spreading, holes. The 'brandy' had burned right through the cloth. After that, we settled for coffee.

I never grew tired of the atmosphere of mild wickedness that one found in the speakeasies, where illicit liquor could be bought. Frequently, there were raids by the police, but never, it seemed, before there had been a tip-off; perhaps this had something to do with the fact that most bars had a kind of grace-and-favour seat for the local cop. As soon as the red light lit up in the speakeasy, the booze would vanish with amazing speed through concealed trapdoors.

New York then seemed a city where anything was possible. One weekend, a party of us, including Evelyn Laye, who was playing in *Bitter Sweet* at the Ziegfeld Theatre, decided to go skiing at Brier Cliff, just outside New York. Because we were going by train, the timing for this expedition was pretty fine.

To attempt to get from mid-New York to Grand Central Station through the chaos of Saturday night traffic with only minutes to spare was a pretty hazardous undertaking. Anyway, as my play ended earlier than *Bitter Sweet*, it was decided that I would pick up Boo (Evelyn Laye) at the Ziegfeld. I arrived just as the curtain was going down. Boo rushed into her dressing-room, tore off her stage clothes, and changed.

We arrived at the stage door at a run, calling for a taxi, but instead were met by a couple of policemen. They grabbed our luggage, and said: 'This way, please.'

To our astonishment, we were bundled into a huge limousine, flanked by motor-cycle outriders, and led by a police car. With lights flashing and sirens wailing, we streaked through the traffic and arrived at the station with ten minutes to spare.

This was the first time in my life that this had happened. The second—and last—was under horrifying circumstances in 1973—when in a pool of blood I was rushed by ambulance to hospital with a police escort.

Towards the end of the first year's run of *Journey's End*, Larry Olivier arrived in New York, with a not very successful play by Frank Vosper called *Murder on the Second Floor*. He was going through a bad patch, first with the failure of *Beau Geste*, followed by a not very lucrative run of *The Chalk Circle*, and now this thriller was also doomed to die. But he always remained in good spirits, and as ever he was a splendid companion. He consoled himself with the company of an extraordinary dog that he bought from a man in the street. The animal reminded me of two extremely dirty brown face flannels knotted together, but Larry assured me it was a very rare Portuguese Wolf Hound. Sadly, it had to go because it developed an addiction to bathtub gin and was constantly fainting.

There was a kind of madness in the air of New York that autumn—the atmosphere that bred alcoholic dogs, perhaps. The great October crash was just around the corner, and the warning whispers of the impending crisis had risen to a steady rumble. Even so, few people took the situation seriously: prophets of doom are invariably disregarded. I suppose it was the same in the last days before Pompeii.

The theatres and night-clubs were still packed, and it seemed as though people felt that if they ignored the situation it might just go away. I, too, was feeling restless, and worse still, I was in love. An extremely beautiful young English actress whom I had known from the Italia Conti days arrived in another British production. This was not a success, but in the four weeks before it folded, she and I thought we were passionately in love.

When she and her defeated company returned to London, I was in despair. This, I felt sure, was the definitive love of my life. I had to follow her, so I went to the management to plead for a release. It was granted with almost indecent alacrity, and I was replaced that same day by an actor who was paid about a third of the salary I had been earning.

Apart from a punishing round of farewell parties, there was one final episode that typified the America of those days. In order to get my exit permit, I had to have a certificate that showed I had paid all my American income tax, before I could leave. The inevitable 'Mr. Fixit' fortunately appeared on the scene. He told me to ring a certain tax official and make an appointment. When I sat down in his office, I was told that I would see an open drawer in his desk. Into this I should drop a fifty-dollar bill.

Everything happened just as it had been described. The drawer was open, and into it I dropped the folded bill. The man closed the drawer, not even glancing down at it. Then he opened a folder on his desk.

'Mr Hawkins, I see that you have an invalid mother and a retired father whom you support?'

Before I could deny this, he listed an amazing catalogue of commitments on my salary. In the end I paid 250 dollars tax, just over one week's salary. And I had been earning 200 dollars a week for over a year! I must say I did not object, and I did attempt to answer the questions correctly, but the official just put other and more convenient answers into my mouth.

At least, I had made enough money in New York to be able to put down a hefty deposit on a house for my parents at Winchmore Hill, North London, and was well enough off to guarantee their mortgage. But my love life was not as successful. Just as soon as I returned to London I telephoned my little actress, and we met in the bar of the Arts Theatre Club. As she walked up to meet me, I knew I had made a terrible mistake. Fortunately for both of us, she had taken a job with a touring company, and the affair fizzled out as quickly as it had started.

Once again I was out of work, and felt more than a little foolish for having abandoned a starring part in a highly successful play to come home to—nothing.

# FOUR

Since I had rather precipitately put my whole career in jeopardy, I decided that the time had come to step aside and quietly take stock of what I had achieved and where I was going.

After the frenetic life of New York I found Winchmore Hill a soothing and very quiet contrast. Here were no cliff-like buildings, no concrete canyons, but fields—yes, there were fields in Winchmore Hill then—and the woods that surrounded the house I had bought for my parents had been a favourite childhood haunt of mine.

With my friends in St Michael's choir I had fished the ponds for newts and tadpoles, and now all I wanted was to recapture those untroubled days and try and work out my future. I had some money in my bank account, and so I felt I could afford a break from work. As things turned out, I had little time for country walks, for about two weeks after I returned home I was called to an interview with Somerset Maugham and Ronald Squire, and offered a part in a new Maugham play—*The Breadwinner*—with Marie Lohr and Peggy Ashcroft.

Ronnie was playing the lead, a Gauguin-like character who abandons his family and respectable business career to do what now would be called 'his own thing'.

The director was a rather blimpish actor-producer, an individual who had a huge sense of humour, but little tact that I could see. Somerset Maugham, since his death, has been credited with an unpleasant, waspish nature, but I grew to know him quite well and always found him to be scrupulously polite and courteous.

Unlike Shaw, who would have liked not only to have directed his plays, but to have the acted the parts as well if he could have pushed his way on to the stage, Somerset Maugham never interfered with rehearsals.

I remember very well one instance of Maugham's kindness. We were having a pre-London run in Eastbourne, which was marred on the first night when the director strongly criticised a young actress, Margaret Hood, who for the first time in her career was playing with a very experienced West End cast.

The poor girl was reduced to tears, and when the rest of us went off to the opening night dinner party that Maugham had generously arranged, she remained sobbing in her dressing-room. While we were all sipping our aperitifs, Maugham suddenly asked in his strange stammering voice: 'Wh-where's the little g-g-girl?'

Somebody said: 'I think she's still at the theatre.'

'Wh-why?'

'She was a little upset.'

Maugham frowned and immediately sent his chauffeur to collect Maggie, and before she arrived he asked the director what had upset her. The man admitted he had given her a roasting, and Maugham, putting on his most chilling, mandarin face, said that if he interfered with the cast again, the management would lose the performing rights of the play.

Maggie arrived, red-eyed and miserable, but Willie placed her on his right at the dinner table, and spent the rest of the evening treating her as though she was the leading lady. In fact, the play was not very well received in London, but even so it ran for five months, and when it came off I still had a year to run on my contract with Basil Dean. So that I should not be idle, he sent me the script of a play called *Solitude* by a new playwright, one C. L. Anthony. I did not know whether this was a man or a woman, but eventually when the play was renamed *Autumn Crocus*, I discovered that C. L. Anthony was a funny little girl, a buyer at Heal's department store, named Dodie Smith.

The play opened disastrously on an Easter Monday. Such first-night fiascos were by no means uncommon then. The galleryites had decided that they could be arbiters of taste in the theatre, simply by raising their voices loudly enough, regardless of the

43

merits of the play. This was an early example of mass power; already Ivor Novello had had one of his plays virtually booed off the stage, and Noël Coward's *Sirocco* had been reduced to a shambles.

All went well with us until we lined up to take our bows, and then the gallery erupted to shouts of 'Rubbish!', 'Take it off!' At this, people in the stalls turned on the gallery, yelling:'You're idiots! You don't know what you're talking about! Get out of the theatre.'

This was the first time I had ever come up against such a demonstration, and we all felt complete fools standing on the stage while this terrific verbal battle was being fought in the auditorium. Finally, the curtain came down and muffled the demonstration, and Basil Dean came on to the stage looking utterly disconsolate.

'Thank you, my dears,' he said. 'You all did splendidly. I am sorry it has ended like this.' In fact, this was only the beginning— the play ran for eighteen months!

This also marked the start of one of the most marvellous summers of my life. In the cast of *Autumn Crocus* was a splendid actor, Arthur Hambling, who was playing the part of a clergyman.We became friends immediately because we were both very keen fishermen and loved the Thames. In our spare time we used to hire a punt and spend the day fishing on the river and its tributaries, and usually we would wind up the day at a lovely pub, *The Angler's Rest*, at Bell Weir, Egham, just above Staines.

One evening we were downing a few pints, when Arthur said: 'Why don't we camp down here for the rest of the summer?' This seemed a lovely 'Wind in the Willows' idea, and when the publican joined in the conversation and said we could pitch our tents in the field next to his pub for half-a-crown a week, we decided that this was for us. I must say I still had some doubts, but Arthur's enthusiasm was boundless.

We bought two surplus army tents for £10, oil lamps, pots and pans, and a paraffin cooker. The two tents were tacked together, one for sleeping quarters and the other for cooking. We also bought a second-hand punt for £4. Except when we had matinees, on Wednesdays and Saturdays, we used to jump into my car after each evening performance, roar down, on virtually traffic-free roads, to our riverside retreat, and sleep to the sound of the water tumbling over the weir.

I remember this as a golden summer, when the sun shone every day, although the weather must have been typically British, because I discovered a newspaper cutting the other day that said: 'During the run of *Autumn Crocus*, Jack Hawkins and Arthur Hambling have been going down every night after the show to their country house. This is a tent perched on the river bank at Bell Weir, where they have been camping, despite the summer.'

Time is a strange thing looking back, events that seemed so vivid and real at the time shrink in perspective so that one seems to see them through the wrong end of a telescope.

After the Second World War, I drove back to the river bank and stayed with dear old Arthur. I was filming at Shepperton and Dee at Denham and we used to visit him regularly.

Arthur had married and found real contentment in the simple life, but I did not envy him. I was too ambitious, too intent on the bright lights, too eager to be what I considered a success to want to stay in such a backwater.

Looking back, I suppose Arthur was really a hippy before his time—possibly we both were. This realisation has given me sympathy with young people of my children's generation who have turned aside from the strictly materialistic values of life to seek some simpler and, to them, more satisfying way of living.

It always amuses me to see the expression on my friends' faces when they see my elder son drifting through our penthouse flat in his old jeans and sandals. When I was his age, we had to have a far stricter discipline, because life itself was harder; but maybe in our hearts we would have behaved as the young people do today had we been able to do so.

Anyway, at the time, we both enjoyed the change from London, and because Arthur was superbly skilled in country craft, he made our bijou residence very comfortable. On weekends, we

45

used to persuade our various girl-friends to join us. Two of us would sleep in the tent and the other two in the punt, which had a rather cunning canvas cover that fitted over iron hoops. It was rather like sleeping in a canvas tunnel. Behind our tents were an ancient couple, and their aged bachelor son—the father and son worked at the local gas works—and they occupied an extraordinary collection of tumbledown shacks, a beautifully carved circus caravan and an old railway carriage.

While we were there, the old woman was taken ill and whipped into hospital, and the council decided to rehouse the father and son. This was far too good an opportunity to be missed, and so we bought the whole ramshackle collection for £40. They were all in a terrible state of squalor, and for the next few weeks we spent every spare moment on a tremendous task of restoration. We tore down the worst of the shacks, and converted the railway carriage into an elegant drawing-room, with a kitchen, and even made a lovely garden. I took over the caravan for my sleeping quarters.

The one problem was that we had no room for a garage for my car, and in those days cars were more valued possessions than they are today and rarely lived in the open air. This preyed on our minds, until one night, after our usual intake of pints, we hit on the solution. With great stealth, and in pitch darkness, we uprooted our boundary fence and claimed another ten feet of land. Nobody seemed to notice our territorial expansion, so we built our garage on the land we had thus acquired. We found that the river was a very useful source of furniture. If you take the trouble to look, the Thames is still a wonderful depository of unwanted property.

Our best find came on a day when we were punting up a little backwater in search of good fishing pools. I happened to glance over the side, and saw a dark shape on the bed of the stream.

'What the hell's that, Arthur?' I asked.

He peered over the edge.

'A bath,' he said.

Well, a bath was the one thing we didn't have, for we had used the running water of the river, but the problem was how we were going to pull it out of the stream. Our efforts to manhandle it into the punt were a failure, so we went home for ropes and swimming costumes. Eventually, we ran ropes under the bath and hauled it aboard the punt, which we had braced across the narrow stream. It was a bit muddy, but apart from that the bath was in perfect condition.

We had to carry out another midnight land grab to make room for a bathroom, which we built. Arthur managed to find a geyser which worked on paraffin, and so we now had hot running water as well as cold. Living in this eccentric jumble of buildings was undoubtedly one of the happiest periods of my life, only made possible I think by the friendship between Arthur and myself. Although we shared virtually everything, we never allowed it to intrude on one another's lives.

In the mornings, we would split up the household chores, pack fishing gear and lunch into the punt, decide where we were going, and then probably not have more than five minutes' chat for the rest of the day. There was no question of having to make conversation, because we were both entirely engrossed and happy in what we were doing.

I certainly had plenty to think about, because it was during *Autumn Crocus* that I met Jessica Tandy, the girl who was to become my first wife.

We were playing the young lovers in the play who were living together, or in sin, as Dodie Smith would have it. We were both twenty-one, and tremendously attracted to one another, and I suppose it was inevitable that the parts we were playing on the stage should spread over into real life. At any rate, we became lovers in fact, and rather vaguely talked about marriage, but looking back I don't think we were really in love, although we loved one another's company.

After we left *Autumn Crocus*, Jessica went into repertory with the Cambridge Arts Theatre. I used to go up to see her in some of the productions, and I remember one weekend going with John Gielgud and Frank Vosper to see her in a farcical musical, *Daughter of the Regiment*. It was the dress rehearsal, which pleased Johnnie G.,

47

Frank and me because it meant there was time during the extended interval for us to dine in the splendid little restaurant at the Cambridge Arts. We took a couple of bottles of wine back to the stalls with us, and despite the horrors of the piece, we thoroughly enjoyed ourselves. Jessica, too, seemed in high spirits, but when I saw her the following weekend she was very down in the mouth. It turned out that the director of the frightful musical had taken a terrific shine to her, and was generally making her life intolerable.

Full of youthful gallantry, I said: 'We'll put a stop to this— we'll get engaged', and off we went into Cambridge and bought two platinum rings to mark the occasion. Even so, this did not quite solve the problems. Shortly afterwards, Jessica got the part of Manuela in the German play *Children in Uniform*, and since she was playing a girl of fifteen the management producing the play said that it was impossible for her to get married.

This made us even more determined. I took out a special licence and succeeded in getting into a muddle over the churches, with the result that the Press photographers went to a church in Southgate, while we were married at a Winchmore Hill church. An *Evening News* show columnist, The Stroller, grew very cross at this because he thought we were deliberately trying to snub him.

Jessica's mother was distressed less by losing a daughter than by the fact that when I knelt at the altar rails she spotted a hole in the sole of one of my shoes.

She was an odd woman in many ways. On the night before our wedding she said to Jessica: 'I suppose it's too much to hope that you won't have any sexual connection with Jack?'

Frankly, it was. I often thought afterwards about this peculiar request. I could only come to the conclusion that it was because she had spent most of her life teaching mentally handicapped children and had some weird idea that we would produce an idiot child. Hardly a flattering thought!

As it was, we had an enchanting baby daughter, Susan. I was devoted to my first child, and at the time I little thought that I would only enjoy her company for seven years.

Anyway, after the wedding, we dashed from the church for a quick lunch at Kettners in Soho so that Jessica would be in time for her matinee. I spent the afternoon playing cards at the Green Room Club. We both had evening shows, so it was not until late on that Saturday night that we set off in my little cream Wolseley Hornet for our honeymoon—one night at Great Fosters at Egham.

It was also around this time that I had my first real film part. This was in a film made at the old Twickenham Studios, and it was called *The Lodger*, one of Hitchcock's earliest films. Years later I returned, as a producer, to make *The Ruling Class* with my friend Peter O'Toole. I had appeared in one film before, with a part which was literally two coughs and a spit, and I discovered that I suffered from terrible camera shyness. As soon as I went on the set I developed a frightful nervous twitch that made my face twist into fearful grimaces. I found that the only way to control this was to take aspirin. However, by the end of *The Lodger* I was able to control it unaided.

I was playing opposite Elizabeth Allan, one of the most beautiful young women I have ever seen. She became a close friend, and married Bill O'Bryen, a partner in London's top firm of theatrical agents, who has played a great part in shaping my career.

When I was drawing my £8 a day during the month I was filming, I little thought that in future years I would be earning £100,000 a year. After all, at a time when the average weekly wage in Britain was £2.10s, £8 a day was a princely sum indeed.

At the time of *The Lodger* I was in a very funny, thick-ear farce, which had been written by a young naval commander, Anthony Kimmins. Apart from being a tremendous success, the play was also regarded as being fearfully naughty, almost blue. I played a rather awful, breezy young naval officer, and consequently had most of the so-called blue lines. There was tremendous tut-tutting when I referred to something as being 'better than a slap in the belly with a wet fish', and when I said that my brother (in the play) Greville was 'having a bit of something with Lady Cattering', there were gasps of horror.

49

Of course, now it all seems very tame and harmless compared with the modern theatre with its four-letter words, full frontal nudity, and simulated sex, but it packed in the audiences. About the best thing that came out of the play was the very close friendship that developed between myself and Hugh Williams. Tam, as we all called him, became one of my closest friends.

I remember the terrible panic we both got into on the opening night of *While Parents Sleep*. We were in the Green Room Club, having a drink and a sandwich before going to the theatre. As usual, it was packed with actors, and there was the normal chorus of 'Hullo, have a drink', and then 'Have another'. We said, 'No, we mustn't have any more, we've got a first night.'

There was a rather nasty silence, and then someone asked bluntly: 'What first night?'

'OUR first night,' we replied proudly.

'Oh. What's the play called?'

It was quite clear that nobody knew anything about our play, and if actors don't know of a new play, then there is precious little chance of the theatre-going public being aware of it.

By the time we arrived at the Royalty in Dean Street—now, alas, an office block—we were both deeply depressed, in a frightful state of nerves, quite convinced that it was going to be the biggest flop of all time. I decided something had to be done, and in spite of Tam's protests I sent my dresser across to the Quo Vadis, my favourite restaurant, for a bottle of champagne and two glasses. By the time we had polished off the bottle we both felt a good deal better about the situation. In fact, the first night was a roaring success, largely because there can have been few plays with so many backers, and they were all there.

What had happened was Leon M. Lyon, who owned the Royalty—the play was directed by Sir Nigel Playfair, who also acted in it—had been unable or unwilling to raise all the money for the production. He had told Anthony Kimmins that he would stage the play, providing he raised about £750.

So Anthony went back to his naval mess and asked all his friends to chip in what they could afford, with the result that dozens of 'angels' and their girl-friends and wives turned up for the first night.

Leon, who was extremely clever, scattered them throughout the auditorium so that it seemed as though the entire audience was rooting for the show. I think their enthusiasm was infectious, because the next day we got a marvellous Press, and the play ran for months. My agent at this time, who also got me into films, was Sidney Jay, the archetype of a Jewish actor's agent. He had a rather basic office—where I was acting in the evenings. Dead on 7.30, when I was making up, he would arrive in my dressing-room, and say: 'How did it go today, Jack boy?'

I'd reply, 'Fine'. Then he would go over to the hand-basin and say: 'You don't mind if I wash me hands?'

It took a little while to realise that he only called to have a wash and brush-up on his way home. I don't think that his office had such facilities.

Another of the most regular backstage visitors during the run of the play was the old Duke of Marlborough, the grandfather of the present Duke, who was extremely keen on the very beautiful Canadian actress, Frances Doble. I think she found him a little heavy on the hand, because whenever he called she would always invite Tam and I to her dressing-room for a drink, and a chat with the old boy.

I remember one evening—I was still in my make-up, greasepaint called five and nine, which gave one a kind of Red Indian complexion—and he kept peering at my face until I began to wonder if I was coming out in a rash, or had a pimple on my nose. Eventually, his curiosity got the better of him.

'Tell me, my boy, does it sting much to put all that iodine on your face?' he asked.

Apart from being enormous fun to act in, the play was made enjoyable for me by Hugh's presence. Urbane, clever, and extremely amusing, he was a delightful companion, and we spent a great deal of time together.

Shortly after he got married he was introduced to Tallulah Bankhead, and like most other people, including myself, he was

51

completely bowled over by her. She appeared to be equally infatuated. The situation became increasingly difficult, and his family and friends decided that the time had come for drastic action. It was decided that he should go on a tour of Australia. At the same time Tallulah's friends were doing all they could to prevent him leaving. Tam became quite desperate.

One evening in the Green Room Club, when he had had a good deal too much to drink, he told me that he had decided to end it all. This, he was convinced, was the only solution. I didn't take him very seriously because I was convinced he was far too sophisticated to contemplate suicide. We parted company quite late that night, with Tam saying that he was going to walk home to his house in Well Walk, Hampstead. Later, he told me that when he reached Whitestone Pond he made up his mind to end his life. He paused on the edge for a moment, and then took a great leap into the black water.

What he didn't realise was that nowhere in the pond is the water more than eighteen inches deep. He said he felt distinctly foolish when he found himself on his hands and knees in only a few inches of water, so he paddled out and went home with nothing worse than wet clothes and bruised knees. His affair with Tallulah ended in this famous watering hole of the Royal Horse Artillery.

During the six years up to the start of the Second World War, I appeared in a number of plays that ranged from farce to Shakespeare.

I played Jack Maitland in The Maitlands, Horatio in Hamlet, and travelled to Elsinore to play the King in the same play as well as appearing in comedies like Accidentally Yours and Indoor Fireworks. I was Benedict in Much Ado, Caliban in The Tempest and also appeared in a memorable production of Milton's Comus. I sailed to New York to star in Dear Octopus, and frequently was also working in films in Britain. I do not remember all of these, for like many actors in those days I did not take my films very seriously. One tended to regard them as second-rate compared with the live theatre—which in many cases was quite true—and little more than a means of paying one's income tax. I never imagined that my greatest fame would be earned on the screen.

I did act with some marvellous people, though, and I remember Anna Neagle and I making a mildly ridiculous period piece called *Peg of Old Drury*. It was fairly fraught because we would all turn up at the crack of dawn to be made up and dressed, only to hang around for hours waiting for something to happen. It was only later that I discovered that Herbert Wilcox, who was producing and directing, was running into terrible financial problems over the film, and was spending half the time he should have been at the studio chasing around the City trying to raise money.

I still had every reason to believe that my fame would be found on the stage, and I recall J. G. Bergel, the dramatic critic of the *Evening News*, when he was predicting who would become the male stars of the theatre, writing in 1933: 'Perhaps they will all be outstripped in the end by Mr Jack Hawkins, who is only 23. Mr Hawkins looks like training to be the irresistibly breezy, infectiously gay young hero—something, if you can imagine it, midway between Mr Jack Hulbert and Mr Owen Nares, and the most indubitable of matinee idols.'

The other names on his list included Robert Donat, Ralph Richardson, Frank Vosper, Edward Chapman and John Gielgud. So at least I was in good company.

In 1935, I was picked to act with George Robey in an idiotic French farce at the Theatre Royal, called *Accidentally Yours*. George Robey taught me more about playing comedy than anyone else. I had been a devoted fan of his ever since, as a child actor, I had watched him perform at the Holborn Empire. His sense of timing was magical, but he had a disconcerting habit of suddenly ad libbing. One of his favourite ploys was to tell a slightly dirty story just before going on the stage, and then slip the tag line unexpectedly into the dialogue. Of course, the wretched audience had no idea what was going on, but the supporting actor would be thrown into a state of disarray.

One evening, just as we were about go on, he drew me to one side to tell what he thought was a funny story.

53

'Jack,' he began, 'did I ever tell you the one about two land-ladies discussing their guests? One said to the other: "I see you have a coloured gentleman staying with you. What's he like?"

'The other replied, "Oh, he's very nice, very polite. No trouble at all. But there is one funny thing about him. The other day I heard him fart, and when I went into his room it was full of soot."'

In the play, I took the part of a young novelist madly in love with George's stage mistress, played by Alice Delysia, and in this particular scene my exit line was: 'I must write all this down. Is there a room I can use?'

George replied: 'Go in there, but be careful, there's a coloured gentleman in the room and the place is full of soot.'

Although George was a master of the innuendo—one heave of his huge black-painted eyebrows could give even the most inno-cent line a thoroughly dubious meaning—he was at heart a puritan. In *Accidentally Yours* he was expected to use the word 'bloody', and only after endless persuasion did he agree to use it, although in ordinary conversation it was his most frequent expletive. I think he was a frustrated violinist, and spent most of his spare time making violins. Often irascible and tetchy, he was at heart a very simple man. I remember he took a touching pride in the OBE he was awarded for his work for charity, and would carry it around in his briefcase to show to people. He liked to build up stories around the presentation by King George V.

When he showed it to me, he explained: 'When the King handed me the order he said: "Have you heard any good ones, George?" So I told him a nice brisk one, and as I was bowing to him, Queen Mary turned to the King and asked: "What was Mr Robey telling you?" So he told her the story, and she said: "Disgusting! You shouldn't have given him the bloody medal!"'

Somehow, I seemed to attract disaster when I was rehearsing for plays. There was the awful incident with the lance in *St Joan*, and the damage I caused with the Maxim gun in *Beau Geste*, but it was while rehearsing the stage version of Edgar Wallace's thriller, *The Frog*, that I nearly got killed. I was playing a detective, and in one scene a mysterious gang of criminals try to blow up my office, with the effect of a huge wooden shutter at the window behind my desk being blasted out. During the dress rehearsal one of the ropes that operated the effect broke. The shutter fell on to me, and I took the full weight on the back of my head. I was knocked out cold, but fortunately recovered in time to take part in the opening. I was knocked out once more by my wife's remarks after the opening.

'How can you forgo the classical theatre just to make money?' she asked contemptuously.

All very well, I thought, but someone had to make enough to support our house in Hampstead and our daughter. So, happily, *The Frog* did have a very long run, and then I made the film version.

Even so, the parts that gave me the greatest pleasure during this period were in Shakespearean productions. I worked with John Gielgud a great deal, but for sheer fun nothing quite equalled the Regent's Park open-air productions. This extraordinary venture was started by Sidney Carroll, the theatre critic of *The Daily Telegraph*, who became quite obsessed and besotted with the Regent's Park theatre.

They were very traditional productions of Shakespeare, and, when the weather was good, which was not too often, they were quite lovely to look at. Sidney employed very good verse speakers, but they tended to be of the old-fashioned school, like the very grand and dramatic actress Phyllis Neilson Terry. I think I was invited in order to introduce something of the then modern school of acting.

Robert Atkins was the producer, a peculiar shabby-looking old character, with a wonderfully round, rich voice, and a habit of abusing everyone in a rich strain of invective.

I remember him one day, standing on the huge grass amphitheatre, always known as the Greensward, roaring at us: 'Take some bloody interest! I don't want you standing around looking like a lot of bloody old newspapers that have been out in the rain all night.' Unfortunately someone had left the loudspeakers on, and his tirade bellowed out over the park. We could see the nannies grabbing their charges and fleeing out of earshot.

Of course, putting on an open-air production was always a hazardous undertaking. As anyone who has been to the open-air theatre will know, the heavens invariably open half-way through the performance, and both audience and actors have to make a dash for the covered theatre. It was weird acting under cover because there was a slight gap between the stage tents and the marquee where the audience sat, through which the rain poured, so one was cut off by a kind of curtain of water.

As soon as the rain cleared, we all raced back into the open, by which time the Greensward was sopping wet and incredibly slippery.

Because the stage was so large, about ninety feet across, instead of taking a normal line-up bow, we used to cavort in a kind of daisy chain across the front, and around the bushes at the back. If you happened to be at the end of the chain, by about the third time round you were moving at a terrific speed.

I particularly remember one evening when I was the penultimate link in the chain, with Phyllis Neilson Terry at the end. As usual there had been a downpour half-way through, and the surface was like a skating rink. On the second circuit poor Phyllis, who was wearing a kind of long white wedding gown right down to her feet, slipped and fell. I couldn't just abandon her, neither could I let go of the chain, so I towed her along on her backside into the bushes. Not the most dignified exit ever made by one of the *grande dames* of the English stage.

But throughout those last few years before the war I always seemed to gravitate back to John Gielgud. I first worked with him in his production of *Richard of Bordeaux*, when I took over the part of the Earl of Oxford from Francis Lister. A few months after I joined, the production celebrated its first anniversary, and of course there were a large number of *aficionados* at the front of the house.

At the end of the performance there were cries of 'Speech, speech!' and Johnny stepped forward. He thanked the audience

At twelve years, as
Ruth in *The Pirates
of Penzance*

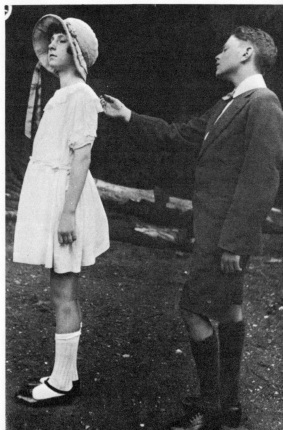

At about the same age,
in one of the amateur
theatrical productions
which was to lead me
on to Conti's

Aged thirteen, playing Dunois's page in *St. Joan*
with Sybil Thorndike

As Hibbert in
*Journey's End* when
I was eighteen

*De Mirjian Studio*

The following year,
in *The Breadwinner*
with Ronald Squire

Early film days (1932):
*The Lodger*, which starred
Ivor Novello and
Elizabeth Allan

*Cyril Stanborough*

In a Regents Park
production of *As You
Like It*, playing opposite
Anna Neagle

Dee in 1944, just after we met out in India

'She started down the stairs: I thought she was calmer.'
A scene with Ralph Richardson in *The Fallen Idol*.
This was 1947, the year of my marriage to Dee

In *The Elusive Pimpernel* in 1948: left to right, Margaret Leighton,
myself, David Niven, Patrick MacNee and Robert Coote

As Tristram in
*The Black Rose* (1949)
which we filmed
in Morocco

Mercutio in
*Romeo and Juliet*
(New York, 1951)

*John Seymour Erwin*

On the set of
*No Highway* with
Marlene Dietrich
in 1951

Location filming for *The Cruel
Sea* (1952), with 'Janky' Clark. The
rum was for protection against
the cold water in and around
the rubber raft!

*Keystone*

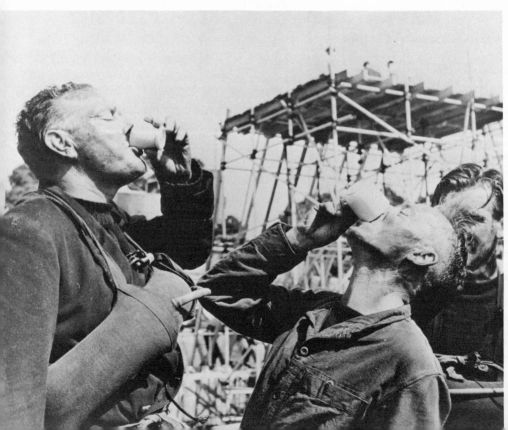

for its support, and said: 'I know that many of you have been to see us thirty or forty times.' He paused, and looked along the line of the cast, searching for words. His eyes lighted on me, and he added: 'In spite of the changes in the cast.'

During the phoney war period in 1940, I toured with Johnny's production of Oscar Wilde's *The Importance of Being Earnest*. It is odd how some plays and parts stay in the mind long after others have been forgotten. This was one of the plays I remember best—which also made such a great impression on those who saw it that I still receive letters from people who were in the audience, either in London or in one of the places we visited on tour, during that far-off spring and summer.

The cast was fantastic: Edith Evans as Lady Bracknell, Peggy Ashcroft, Gwen Ffrangcon-Davies and Margaret Rutherford.

Maybe part of the play's astonishing success stemmed from the fact that somehow that brittle, brilliant period piece reflected the unbelieving, almost frivolous view we all took of the war, and even when it was obvious that this was real war, and no longer phoney, it still had a magic all its own.

Later that summer, a group of us, including my wife Jessica, got together and tried to keep the Old Vic going. In spite of the cast—which I suppose constituted about forty per cent of the best classical actors and actresses in the country—it was soon clear that the attempt was doomed. So was my marriage.

I have listed only some of the plays—and hardly any of the films—in which I appeared in the years just before the war, to show that my private and personal life came a very poor second to my professional career.

Jessica was equally ambitious, and so our relationship, like that of Shakespeare's young lasses, was star-crossed in the most literal sense: we were both too busy seeking to be stars ourselves to have time for marriage. Ambition came between us, and instead of being content to build a home life like so many other young couples of our age, we concentrated on building our careers. Obviously, we steadily grew apart until our marriage was in serious danger. Thus, when Jessica was offered a very good part in

America, it seemed sensible for her to go. I was anxious that our little daughter, Susan, should be somewhere safe, for prospects in Britain did not seem bright in 1940. So they sailed away together. But when we said goodbye in London, I never imagined that ten years would pass before I saw either of them again.

# FIVE

After the fall of France, and the evacuation from Dunkirk, London seemed filled with men and women in uniform. I felt lonely, unhappy and restless. In the harsh excitement of war the make-believe world of the theatre had suddenly lost its appeal. I wanted to be doing something positive, but apparently my services were not required; no call-up papers arrived, no summons to arms of any kind.

One of my fellow actors at the Old Vic, Andrew Cruikshank, now so well known for creating the part of Dr Cameron in BBC-TV's *Dr Finlay's Casebook*, felt much as I did, and we decided to volunteer. But for some extraordinary reason, despite Dunkirk, the War Office had decided that the Army did not require any more volunteers, so I started to cast around for people of influence.

The first I approached was Lord Semphill, whom I had once met socially and whom I believed had something to do with the Royal Navy Air Service.

'Why don't you come into the Navy?' he suggested. I said I didn't know anything about sailing ships.

'That doesn't matter. I expect they'll ask you if you have ever been sailing. You just reply "Yes", and you'll be in.'

That didn't sound very satisfactory to me—especially as I suffered from sea sickness—so I looked up an old friend who was a fellow member of the Savage Club, and who I knew was doing some unspecified job for the War Office. He was not much more encouraging, beyond suggesting that I signed on with a Guards regiment for seven years. Then a week later he telephoned me.

'Don't tell anyone where you got this from, Jack,' he said. 'But if you go to the recruiting centre in Seven Sisters Road in

Holloway you can volunteer for the Royal Welch Fusiliers, the 23rd Foot. For some reason, the order stopping recruiting hasn't got through to that Regiment yet.'

I telephoned Andrew and together we drove down to the recruiting centre in my car. A magnificent recruiting sergeant came over as we drew up, and asked if he could help. We said we had come to volunteer.

'Sorry, gentlemen,' he replied, 'but there's no more volunteering.'

'We've come to volunteer for the Royal Welch Fusiliers,' we explained.

The Sergeant looked as though we had offered him dirty postcards. In a hoarse whisper he asked us to drive round the corner, park the car, and then come back in a few minutes. When we walked into the office he said that the Major in charge was a bit busy, but if we would just walk across the road and have a drink, and come back in half an hour, he would see us. By this time, both Andrew and I began to think we were volunteering for the Secret Service.

When we returned half an hour later, we were hurried past a crowd of half-naked call-up boys, and into the Major's office.

'How did you know about this volunteering?' he demanded.

'A friend of mine said we could volunteer for the 23rd Foot,' I replied.

'That's correct,' he agreed. 'I've had no order rescinding that. You had both better have a medical.'

The medicals took about four minutes a piece, and then we were back in the Major's office taking the Oath of Allegiance and being presented with the King's shilling. I fancy we were among the last soldiers in the war who went through this ceremony, because men who were called up were not required to take the Oath.

We congratulated ourselves on how smoothly everything had gone, but there were more problems and misunderstandings ahead.

A month later, we climbed out of a taxi, with our rather smart luggage, at the gates of the Regiment's barracks at Wrexham.

The guard snapped to attention and shouted out: 'Gentlemen, 'ere!' The sergeant of the guard marched out smartly to meet us.

'Good evening, gentlemen. Come to join us?'

'Yes.'

A soldier was ordered to carry our cases, and we were led into the guard room. Tea was brought, and the Sergeant took our names and said he would just go and see the adjutant.

We were still sipping our tea when the Sergeant returned, looking distinctly agitated, and told us that the adjutant wanted to see us. When we arrived at the adjutant's office a couple of clerks were pulling files out of cabinets and searching through them. They gave us both very old-fashioned looks.

Eventually, the adjutant arrived, a very smooth and rather splendid character, and asked us to sit down.

'There seems to have been a bit of a muddle down the line somewhere,' he said. 'We don't appear to have your papers. When were you asked to report?'

I said we had been given this particular date because I understood that this was when the regiment was expecting a new intake of recruits. Instantly there was a deathly hush.

'An intake of what?'

'Recruits,' I repeated, surprised that he did not seem to know the word.

'Do you mean to say you are not officer cadets?'

I handed over my papers, and he took one look at them.

'Good God! Sergeant!' he shouted. 'Take these men back to the guard room and post them to some billet or other.'

As we were being marched back across the parade ground, the Sergeant snarled at us: 'You've taken the piss out of me, and I shan't forget it in a hurry.'

Equipment of any kind was very hard to come by. We were issued with a sort of denim uniform, a rifle and that was about all. Physical training every morning before breakfast—which was absolute torture—included gas-mask drill twice a week by order of Western Command. We wretched recruits only had our civilian masks, which consisted of a rubber face-piece fitted with an unmanageable filter-box at the end. These were no doubt admirable for sedentary jobs, but most unsuitable for violent exercise. Naturally, as the instructors were regular soldiers, they had been issued with army gas-masks, good solid jobs that were strapped to the chest.

When they gave the command, 'Running on the spot—begin!' they were in splendid shape, but the rest of us looked, and felt like, semi-trunked elephants, and the effort of the violent exercise, thus accoutred, was shattering.

One day in the barrack-room, I noticed a recruit on the opposite bunk having a vigorous one-two-three with a knife on his gas-mask. I wandered over and asked politely what the hell he was doing.

'I'm not putting oop wit this bloody lot any longer!' he replied.

When he had split the rubber half-way round the container, he slipped it on his head and said with remarkable clarity, 'That's bloody better! Now I can breathe!' Obviously a soldier of genius.

When we had the next gas-mask session, on the command to don masks, about half the platoon produced a wonderful display of gaping holes. The Sergeant had to remove his splendid model in order to inquire what the bloody hell was going on.

He stopped in front of me. I explained politely, but firmly, that I felt that the designers of the civilian masks had not envisaged the possibility of their getting the bashing they were being subjected to during this violent exercise.

'Right, Hawkins!' the Sergeant exclaimed. 'Go to the Quarter-master's Stores and see what can be done about it!'

I put on my denims and went to the main building of the barracks. On finding the Q.M. stores, I went in. A tiny, round, red-faced captain was wandering along a sort of no-help-yourself counter.

'Well, what is it?' he barked.

'Sir,' I said saluting so fiercely that I nearly knocked myself out. 'Gas-masks!'

He looked at me as if I had asked for the Crown Jewels.

'Gas-masks? You've got a bloody hope, my boy.'

'But, sir,' I stammered. 'Mine is broken.'

'Yes, but that's a civilian one.'

'Then, do I get another from the civilian authorities, sir?'

'Don't be a B.F.: you're in the Army, and the Army will supply you with all necessities. Unfortunately, we are not in a position to help you at the moment! So, piss off.'

The crunch came that evening. A few of us were going to the local pub for a beer, and, as was customary, we had to pass through the guardroom so that the sergeant of the guard could satisfy himself that we were properly dressed.

'You!' he said to me. 'Where's your gas mask. You know they 'ave to be carried at all times!'

'I'm sorry, Sergeant, it's broken,' I explained.

'That doesn't matter. Go and get it!'

So, on returning to the guardroom, a cardboard box containing some shreds of rubber was my passport to a pint of bitter.

After Andrew and I had completed our three months' basic training, we were picked out as 'officer material'.

I approached my pre-OCTU selection board with some misgivings, because I couldn't say that I had been to Eton or Oxford; I couldn't even claim to have been to RADA. So far as the board was concerned I was just one of those 'actor chappies', and I could see when they started questioning me that they were not overimpressed. Then one of the officers asked me what I did in my spare time. I said that I was very fond of riding, and had kept my own hunter.

I used to ride to point-to-points, until the day I was thrown and the management of the theatre where I was playing forbade me to ride in case I was seriously injured.

A couple of the old characters pricked up their ears at that.

'Did you hunt?' one of them asked hopefully.

'Yes. I used to go out with the Smith Bosanquet Hunt from Theobald's Park.'

I had spent many a day in the saddle when, just after my

63

marriage and before moving to Hampstead, Jessica and I had lived in Enfield, then right out in the country.

'You used to hunt with old Smith Bosanquet? How splendid.' And I was in.

Once I joined that Officer Training Corps at Pwllheli in North Wales I began to regret that I had not remained a private soldier. The conditions in this little town were abysmal. Our arrival more or less trebled the population, and the facilities were virtually non-existent. We were billeted on very reluctant landladies, who in happier times ran small boarding houses. There was a permanent shortage of food, and one was constantly hungry on a tedious diet of rabbit stew.

Fortunately, because of the shortage of officers following Dunkirk, the training period was cut to ten weeks, and because of the shortage of equipment, we had to train with wooden models of mortars and anti-tank guns, both then totally inadequate weapons. Andrew and I had to guard the Beddgelert Pass against all invaders.

My army career was nothing if not unusual. About three months after being commissioned as a second lieutenant, I was summoned to the War Office and told that I had been seconded to make a propaganda film about security, called 'Next of Kin'.

I was delighted to be getting back to a bit of acting, and the thought of being able to supplement my officer's pay of eleven shillings a day with an acting fee was very attractive. But when I mentioned the question of salary, this very charming man at the War Office threw up his hands.

'Dear me, no,' he said. 'You've been seconded. You'll be on your normal pay.'

As I was staying at the Savage Club I asked about billeting only to be told that the War Office did not billet people.

'But,' he said, 'the Savage Club is very convenient. I should stay on there.'

Since the club was costing me one pound a day, and my pay was eleven shillings a day, the future did not look too healthy.

Even more depressing was discovering at the studios that the civilian actors were being paid £15 a day. Dave Hutcheson, an old friend, who had starred with Jack Buchanan in many of his musicals, had also been seconded for the film, and I decided something had to be done. We went to see Michael Balcon, who was producing, and told him our tale of woe.

'My dear boys,' he said, 'I have given my word to the War Office that you will only get your basic army pay.'

'Come on, Mick,' David said. 'Nobody's looking. Just drop a few pounds in here,' and he opened the pocket of his greatcoat. But, of course, nothing was dropped in. It was the lowest-paid engagement I had endured since I started acting as a boy of thirteen. At the end of the film, I rejoined my regiment, up to my neck in debt. But for the kindness of my old friend Gordon Harker, who used to slip me a cheque for £20 from time to time, I would have been sunk.

By the time I returned to proper soldiering again I was feeling fairly disillusioned, but there were worse things in store than starving at the Savage Club. During my absence at Ealing Studios it had been decided to amalgamate the Royal Welsh, the South Wales Borderers and the Welsh Regiment into a single holding depot, and to hand the Wrexham depot over to the ATS.

I was told that I had been picked to carry through the hand-over because of my 'diplomatic manner'. That, at least, was the excuse my commanding officer gave me. I, however, was convinced that this meant I was going to spend the rest of the war in the women's army. Fortunately, this situation only lasted a month before I was posted to the 1st Battalion of the Royal Welsh, who were camped on Cheltenham racecourse.

Bad luck, it is said, runs in cycles of three, and the third blow fell as I was sitting in a loose-box, which I had been given as an office, when a letter from Jessica was delivered by an orderly. It was full of chatty news until the last page, where she simply wrote: 'Darling, I don't want to shock you, but I want a divorce.'

We had gone our own ways, and indeed during the last few years our marriage had meant little more than sharing the same house. Now, it appeared, she had fallen in love with a Canadian, and she wanted to marry him.

That night I went out and got hugely drunk, and as I was staggering back to my quarters in the blackout, I literally fell up against the padre. He helped me into bed, and I poured out my misery to him. The next day I was called to the CO's office and he told me to take a week's leave to sort things out.

Jessica had mentioned the name of a firm of solicitors in London who were acting for her, and I took myself off to see them. It was not an interview I relished, but the partner I saw was extraordinarily sympathetic, and, in the odd way that things often work out, eventually took over all my affairs.

After Jessica's letter I think my sanity was preserved by the fact that we were suddenly posted to India, and at last it seemed that I was to be allowed to do some real soldiering.

Anyway, a year later, deep in the Indian jungle, I received a letter from America, which had been chasing me around for months. The first words that met my eyes were: 'From the State of Nevada—Greetings', and then went on to summon me to appear at a divorce court in Las Vegas on a date that had already passed three months before.

I was thoroughly enjoying myself as second-in-command of a Bren-gun carrier platoon, when the CO—we shared a common interest, a mutual dislike of one another—sent me on a course at a hastily set-up battle school. This was pure hell. We had to go on sixty-mile marches, most of the way through cotton soil, which is like fine powder when it is dry, and adhesive cotton-wool when it is wet. Our supplies on our travels were a wretched goat which we had to slaughter, skin and butcher to make us accustomed to 'living off the land', as the saying of those days described it.

Perhaps because I had been trained to make public declamations, I never ceased voicing my disapproval, until I was finally called in by the officer running the course.

'Hawkins,' he said. 'You're making a bloody nuisance of yourself.'

66

'I'm sorry, but I always say what I feel.'

'Quite right,' he replied. 'That's why I want you to join the staff, and run all the shows for the visiting top brass.'

Well, this seemed a bit like show business, so I jumped at the opportunity. I found a splendid natural amphitheatre just outside Poona, close to where we were billeted, where the visiting military brasshats could sit on their shooting sticks, and watch the troops scurrying around digging trenches and advancing under cover. I used to give a commentary, heavily laced with rude remarks about the top brass, and the whole thing went down very well. It was all pretty theatrical, and ended up with a huge cocktail party for the visitors.

It was at one of these parties that I was asked to step out into the garden to meet General John Grover, the general officer commanding the Second British Division in India. He shook me warmly by the hand and congratulated me on the show. It was good entertainment, he said, just what everyone needed. As we sat out under the trees in the lovely Indian evening, he started to reminisce about the First World War.

'In those days,' he said, 'we had a marvellous concert party called the Cross Keys, and that's the kind of thing we need here for the troops. All they are getting are a few films in a couple of dirty cinemas.'

I agreed that a concert party would be a very good idea.

'I'm glad you think that,' he said. 'Because you are going to run it.'

The following morning he gave me authority to scour the Division for talent, and what was virtually an open cheque on Divisional funds. It was astounding just how much talent was available in the Division. Within six weeks I had assembled a cast, and a large dance band, as well as all the scenery and costumes I needed. So it was less than two months from the meeting in the garden before we opened at the local garrison theatre.

We had no band parts, but they played by ear, and someone scored the various parts. New tunes we picked up from records and broadcasts. My own great starring role was a female

67

impersonation of Carmen Miranda—the first time I had played in drag since Ruth at the age of twelve in *The Pirates of Penzance*.

I wrote the sketches and gags, although I must admit that I shamelessly robbed material from every revue I could remember seeing. The reception to our opening performance was overwhelming; so much so that the army engineers built an astonishing folding stage which we hauled out to camps throughout India, and indeed followed the 14th Army into Burma.

I suppose in a way I regretted not being an active, fighting soldier, but at the same time, probably because I was not a regular, I had a pretty well-developed ambition to remain alive. At any rate, I was quite content to take my concert party around the sub-continent.

It was some months after getting the Cross Keys on the road— we borrowed the name from General Grover's first war concert party and also from the emblem of the Second Division—that I met Eric Dunstan in Bombay. He was a very distinguished broadcaster and journalist, who had been sent to India with an embryonic branch of ENSA. He had virtually no staff, and was fighting for survival.

'I want you with me,' he declared as soon as I explained what I was doing. I was flattered, but rather doubtful that I would get released, but Eric insisted that we went to see General Grover.

'What's in this for Hawkins?' the general asked after he heard him out. 'Will he get promotion?'

'He'll be my second in command,' Eric replied.

'If you give me your word that he gets a majority, you can have him.'

So, thanks to General Grover, I was promoted from being a captain, acting unpaid, to a full major.

Perhaps the gods were on my side, because very shortly afterwards the Second Division was sent to the front line against the Japanese, who were making their big push over the Indian-Burmese frontier, and a great many officers I had known well were lost in the campaign. So, without luck, chance, providence, call it what you will, I could well have ended my war as a corpse in some tangled corner of the Burmese jungle. Instead, I was demobilised with the honorary rank of full colonel. I admit that it still comes as a surprise to me when I receive letters from my regimental association addressed to Col. J. E. Hawkins, in spite of the fact that I have held high rank in every branch of the service since then—but only in action in front of the cameras!

Organising ENSA in India during the war was a comic and sometimes downright depressing business. I don't suppose that even the world's most unsuccessful theatrical agent has ever had to handle quite so many dead-beat acts as were sent to me. We called ourselves the arse-end charlies, for we were at the end of a very long line. So far as the ENSA headquarters in Drury Lane were concerned, we were not only at the bottom of their catalogue of priorities, we WERE the bottom.

All their talents went into finding entertainers for the European theatre of war, starting with the Italian front, and eventually spreading to France and Belgium. After that came the Middle East and various parts of Africa, and finally the flotsam and jetsam no one else wanted would be forwarded to us.

We would receive telegrams from ENSA in London telling us of the imminent arrival of an exciting musical act, but all we would receive would be a lonely pianist who had been deprived of his violinist, or a distraught dancer without her partner. I think what happened was that quite a number of entertainers would wind up in Cairo with a few months of their contracts left to run.

In fact, there was 'a pool' in Cairo of variety performers who had inexplicably become detached from their partners and their parent concert party. Rather than send them back to London, the military authorities would tell them: 'Go to India. You'll love India.' The result, from our point of view in India, was a complete shambles.

One day I received a cable from Cairo announcing the arrival of a repertory company by troopship. I went to Green's Hotel, near the Gateway of India in Bombay, to see who was in this company and what plays they had brought with them.

One of my staff, Major Donald Neville-Willing, who had collected them from the docks, introduced me. The first person I met was a young actress, Doreen Lawrence, a tall fair-haired girl with a lovely figure who in the midst of this shambles appeared completely composed, impressing me immediately. By the time we had finished the first rehearsal of *Private Lives*, in which she played Amanda, I realised two things. One, she was an extremely talented actress and, two, I was greatly attracted to her.

I did not feel that the rest of the Company fell into the same category, but then I discovered that there were good reasons for this. Apparently, they had set out from Liverpool in April 1943, twelve strong with four plays in their repertoire, aboard a troopship destined for Cairo and the Middle East. But, of course, everything was covered in deepest secrecy, and after several weeks of zig-zagging around the Atlantic they unexpectedly landed at Freetown in West Africa.

Nobody was more surprised there than the Entertainments Officer in Freetown, who immediately had to arrange for accommodation for them with private residents. Their presence was an embarrassment, and indeed there was nothing for them to do, so eventually they were loaded into trucks and sent to Accra by road—a distance of 1,200 miles.

Their arrival at Accra was equally unanticipated, and arrangements had to be made for them to be billeted with the RAF. Somewhat bewildered, the wretched company began to wonder when they were going to start the work they had been sent to do, and indeed, why were they in West Africa and not in the Middle East? The explanation of this was that the whole emphasis of the war was shifting, and the armies were beginning to move from the Middle East towards Italy.

After some days of keeping themselves occupied with rehearsals as best they could in RAF quarters, the local town hall was used as a theatre and they were at last able to present their plays. They spent some time in Accra and Army and RAF stations around, then went up to Takoradi where there was a large concentration of South African and British RAF units to be entertained.

Finally, they were flown in a transport plane down to Lagos in Nigeria. By this time, the climate of West Africa and its many hazards, such as malaria, and dysentery, had taken toll, and two members had had to return to England and most of the cast were sick in some way or another, apart from Doreen Lawrence who, as I later discovered, has extraordinary stamina.

Their repertoire was reduced to *Private Lives*—which was the only play with a cast of four. Eventually, what was left of the group boarded a troopship bound for South Africa. They were off-loaded at Durban, again unexpected and an embarrassment to the officers in charge. They then had to wait a month for another troopship to take them on to the original destination—Cairo.

As Doreen told me later, they had no money in South Africa and occupied their time by doing broadcasts; indeed it was only the kindness and hospitality of the people of South Africa that made life bearable.

Finally, they arrived in Cairo to be greeted by an Entertainments Officer who wanted to know why they were there and not in East Africa, which was the only place on the Continent of Africa they had not been! However, in Cairo they managed to replace some of the actors lost through illness and performed *Private Lives* at the Opera House there and at the surrounding camps. It was then that Eric Dunstan persuaded some of them to go to India rather than to the Italian front, so on New Year's Day, 1944, they arrived at Bombay.

When I finally heard their story of woe I realised why I was lumbered with such an odd assortment which included an actor who was deaf in one ear, a stage manager with a wooden leg, and a shell-shocked leading man. I had not realised how decimated the London stage had become of healthy young men—all the fit ones were in the Forces. The rest of the cast consisted of an elderly character lady who had come straight from an amateur company in Devon, and two young actresses, Pamela Roberts and Joanna Duncan.

In the meantime, I went to Poona to borrow some vehicles and saw an amateur production of *Private Lives*. The young officer

71

playing the Noël Coward part was very good, and by borrowing him from his unit I was able to put him, playing Elliott, opposite Doreen in a completely new production of *Private Lives*, which we managed to open in Bombay after only two weeks' hectic rehearsal.

Throughout this time, Doreen maintained a wonderful air of calm while the rest of us felt we were living out some suffocating nightmare, and I think it was this quality that first led us into the relationship that resulted in our marriage.

The opening was one of the nights I will always remember. The play—after all our trials and troubles—was received fantastically well, and Doreen scored a huge personal success. The evening lasted until dawn because Aly Khan gave a party in our honour at his house. This was more splendid than any stage set, for the ceilings were covered with white tuber-roses which have a heady, almost overpowering, scent. French champagne flowed, and the garden leading down to the sea was lit with fairy lights where his private orchestra played on the terrace. All this, in the middle of a war, seemed unreal and dreamlike, and Doreen and I were very happy.

Aly became a very good friend to both of us, and was a most generous and warm-hearted man. Once, for instance, sensing we were working so hard, he arranged a picnic for the whole company at Juhu Beach, several miles out of Bombay. We all arrived expecting a picnic in the English sense with curling dried sandwiches and warm beer, but, no; Aly did everything in the greatest style.

A huge tent was erected on poles, and a magnificent buffet spread out on a huge table with uniformed bearers to wait on us. We drank ice-cold Martinis, and then Aly thought something was lacking.

'Where is the music?' he demanded.

His male secretary apologised for his lack of foresight. He had not thought that His Highness would wish for music, otherwise . . .

Aly cut him short.

'Find some,' he commanded.

The secretary fled away dutifully, and to our immense surprise reappeared fifteen minutes later carrying a gramophone and records.

I asked where he had found them in the middle of a deserted beach.

He shrugged his shoulders.

'I simply went to the nearest house and told them that Prince Aly Khan wanted music, and it was their privilege to supply it.'

The festivities were marred by one incident. Half-way through the party, we heard cries coming from the back of a three-ton lorry. The music stopped, and we rushed to the scene, not knowing what we would find, but certainly not expecting what we did find.

Apparently, the shell-shocked officer had become so overcome by the drink, the music and the whole ambience of luxury that he had persuaded a very lovely, high-born Indian lady to ascend into the truck with him. There, by her account, he had attempted (unsuccessfully) to rape her.

Whether her cries were because of the attempt or because it was unsuccessful, we never discovered. The officer was hustled away in disgrace and posted back to England. The rest of us—including the high-born Indian lady—returned to the party.

After playing in Bombay, I sent the company away on tour, and a stream of entertainers began to arrive—a deluge of fragmented acts; bottom-of-the-bill comedians, contortionists, conjurers, the remains of dancing troupes, strident lady vocalists and booming baritones.

To a man (and woman) they would bounce into my office demanding to be sent to the front line to 'entertain our boys', and invariably they would then add that they did not have much time because they had promised to appear at the Palladium. One had to admire their spirit, but the fact was that the nearest they were ever likely to get to the Palladium was a show at the end of Skegness Pier.

Meanwhile, the army in India was complaining at the lack of entertainment, and we started receiving demands from Drury

73

Lane to explain why we were not providing what they called 'blanket coverage' of India. I think they thought that sending an ENSA party on tour in India was like sending a party from London to Windsor.

Finally, I grew so fed up with their unreasonable complaints that I had a map drawn, superimposing India on the map of Europe, which showed that the distance between Bombay and Calcutta was the same as from London to Moscow. I sent this to the Drury Lane office. It seemed to have the desired effect, because the volume of criticism immediately died away.

Thousands of miles were involved, and we had no transport of our own. I had to spend hours begging lifts, and since the Japs were pressing our troops pretty hard, there was never much room to spare in military transports for knock-about concert parties.

Just to add to the difficulties, Philip Ashley, the young officer I had 'borrowed', went down with dysentery, and I was forced to abandon the tour of *Private Lives* which had been so successful. The now hopelessly reduced rep company hung around in Bombay for a month, before my colonel said: 'We can't have these people sitting around here doing nothing. They'll have to go back to England.'

This was a fearful blow, because by now Doreen and I had grown very close, and the last thing we wanted was to be parted. One night we were having a rather gloomy drink in the Harbour Bar of the Taj Mahal trying to find a way out of the situation, when a great, lanky red-haired character came over to us. It turned out that his name was Dominic Roche, and he was an actor and writer. He and Doreen had met earlier in the war.

We discussed our dilemma with him, and he said that he was only doing clerical work at a transit camp, and couldn't he join the company? This was arranged. All we needed now was one more actor, and we would be back in business. Luckily, the following week another young actor arrived in one of the convoys. I told them both to go away and find a play—but quickly. As though to confirm my colonel's worst doubts about ENSA, yet another concert party arrived. But this one, we were told by the ENSA people in Cairo, was the tops. I took them at their word, and arranged for them to open at the Town Hall in Bombay. The house was packed, for we had spread the word about their excellence.

The show was ghastly, an impresario's nightmare. The singers' voices quavered, and were distinctly off-key; the dancers wobbled on their points, and the comedians' jokes were so frightful that they failed to raise a titter from the entertainment-starved troops. I remember my assistant, Donald Neville-Willing, turning to me when the show reached its full pitch of horror, and in a huge stage whisper, said: 'My God, I feel as though I've got ENSA stitched in sequins on my back.'

After this fiasco I was just about ready to volunteer for any suicide mission into the jungles of Burma, and I have little doubt that my colonel was planning to send me on one, but in the nick of time Doreen and Dominic arrived at my office, and announced that they had found a play. It was a lovely little farce called *Love in a Mist*, which had been a big success in London.

The story concerns two young couples, one on honeymoon and the other on what used to be called a dirty weekend, who are trapped by fog in a lonely farm-house on Dartmoor. They are all desperately trying to get to bed, but are prevented by a series of ridiculous accidents. This was perfect entertainment for sex-starved troops.

We went into rehearsal right away, but on the morning of the day we were to open the newly arrived young actor went down with a violent fever. This time I knew that I could not get away with another cancellation. There was thus nothing for it. I would have to take his place, in spite of the fact that I didn't know the part properly.

I arranged that there would always be somebody sitting by the fireplace on the set with a book on their lap—in fact, a copy of the script—and when I knew I was going to dry up I would stammer on the last line I knew and get over to the fireplace to be prompted. The result was that the stammer gave the dirtiest meaning to

75

even the most innocent lines, and the timing made these even funnier.

The play was a roaring success, and was in constant demand, so much so that the little company worked harder than any other in the Far East. We covered the whole of Central and Eastern India, went south to Ceylon, north to Assam and finally through to Imphal. When the 14th Army drove the Japanese back over the Chindwin River, they were the first entertainers in the battle area.

When I went to visit them in Imphal they were so exhausted that I decided to send them to Assam for a chance to recover, with the result that I got an unnerving signal from General Sir William Slim, who commanded the 14th Army. I remember the words to this day:

'I must protest in the strongest possible terms at your withdrawal of the play company *Love in a Mist*. I insist on its immediate return. Slim.'

I went to GOC headquarters and saw Slim. He was a blunt, but charming man, and eventually agreed that the company needed a rest. But this did not last for long, and they re-joined the 14th Army, and stayed with them right the way through to Mandalay, but without Doreen whom I needed for a new production I had in mind.

During the nine months they had been touring, I had expanded ENSA and moved their headquarters to Calcutta, to be closer to the action, and had acquired a garrison theatre there, where I was able to put on many good productions. By this time we had many excellent performers—from John Gielgud in *Hamlet*, to Edith Evans in *The Late Christopher Bean* to Solomon playing Chopin.

Now I wanted to stage Terence Rattigan's comedy, *While the Sun Shines*, which was actually running in London. I wanted Dee to play Mabel Crumb, and out of another repertory company I was lucky enough to get Angela Dowding and Hugh Latimer, an excellent light comedian, who was seconded from the Army.

This play had been running about three days when we heard that Rangoon was about to fall, and that a massive sea invasion was planned to cut off the Japanese retreat and rearguard. An

76

officer from Mountbatten's headquarters in Ceylon, Stokes Roberts, and I, were discussing this in the bar of the Saturday Club in Calcutta, which was always known as The Slap, when we were joined by a tubby little Air Vice-Marshal, who announced that he had just flown in from China. He had some kind of air liaison job with Chiang Kai-shek, who in those days was the Chinese leader.

'I'm taking my flying boat to Rangoon tomorrow,' the AVM announced. 'Why don't you all come along?'

Maybe it was the drink, but anyway Stokes Roberts and I accepted the invitation. I also thought it would give me an opportunity to grab some decent buildings for ENSA before the army was properly entrenched in the city.

We arrived at the Hooghly River sharp at seven the next morning to join a crowd of about twenty-five other characters. It seemed that our Air Vice-Marshal had been pretty liberal with his invitations, which was a little alarming since the flying-boat was only built for around fourteen passengers. Also, nearly all of us had brought cases of scotch for it seemed unlikely that there would be much to drink in Rangoon.

We were ferried out to the aircraft, the scotch was carefully loaded aboard, and then we climbed in and tried to make ourselves comfortable on a collection of old sacks that had been scattered on the floor. There were no seats, and I must say the pilot looked a bit apprehensive when he saw quite how many people had been packed in.

We chugged down the river for a bit, turned and started the run with all throttles open. Nothing happened. We just bumped along to the end of the run. Back we went and started again. This time, we seemed to hop about a foot into the air, before falling back with a great splash into the water. As we returned for a third attempt, the pilot told our host that he would have to lighten the load, and the only thing he had to dump was fuel. Clearly, he thought our scotch should go instead, but did not like to propose this directly.

'Dump the fuel,' said the Air Vice-Marshal, swiftly.

'But there's nowhere between here and Rangoon to refuel, and we have got to skirt an island that is still held by the Japs,' the pilot explained.

'Never mind,' said the ever-confident Air Vice-Marshal. 'Jettison the fuel.'

So gallons of our fuel ran out into the river—no worries about pollution in those days!—and this time we lurched into the air, just missed the bridge over the Hooghly River, and set off for Rangoon. Amazingly, we arrived over Rangoon without any mishap, and were circling the Irrawaddy, when signals started flashing from the ground.

The pilot turned to the Air Vice-Marshal, who was sitting in the co-pilot's seat, and said: 'They don't want us to land. They say they think the river is mined, and it hasn't been cleared yet. What shall I reply?'

'Nothing,' came the reply. 'We'll pretend we haven't seen the signals. Just take her down.'

Several of us who were strap-hanging just inside the cockpit heard this discouraging exchange, and to a man we wished we were taking our ease with the first drink of the day in The Slap.

Miraculously, we got down and taxied to the bank without hitting anything, although a rather grim-faced party of Military Police was lined up to receive us. I must hand it to the Air Vice-Marshal. Stepping smartly from the flying-boat he looked the MPs squarely in the face and ordered them to take him and his party to the headquarters.

We piled into jeeps and a couple of Japanese army lorries, and rolled up at the one remaining theatre in Rangoon, which had been taken over as a temporary headquarters. Perhaps because I was from ENSA the brigadier in charge wanted to know 'what the hell' I was doing so far ahead of the full force of the 14th Army. I thought that the only possible method of defence in the situation was attack.

'For a start,' I replied imperiously, 'I want this theatre. In addition, I want decent billets for the soldiers under my command, and a good central building as a hostel for my entertainers.'

This seemed to take the wind out of his sails, because he granted

78

all three requests without a murmur. The hostel had a splendid kitchen, and very good rooms, although for some reason most of the basins and loos had been smashed. But when Dee, and the rest of the rep company arrived, she complained rather bitterly when she discovered that the building had last been used as the Japanese officers' brothel.

Quite unplanned drama did seem to follow me around while I ran ENSA in India. In one incident an officer on my staff played a leading, unenviable, but deserved role. For some reason he took a tremendous dislike to a girl who had appeared in a revue we staged in Bombay. Admittedly, she had only a moderate talent, but she wasn't half as bad as he made out. Anyway, he didn't have a good word to say about her, and finally he put it around that she was sleeping with her Indian bearer, which was possibly the worst thing one could say about a European woman living in India in those days.

Inevitably, this remark filtered back to the poor girl, and she wrote to her husband, who was a young Lieutenant-Colonel serving with Wingate in the Chindits.

The ENSA offices at that time were in Green's Hotel in Bombay, and were arranged down one side of the entrance hall in a series of little cubicles. I had one, and this colleague was three doors down from me. I was in my office one morning when the door of the hotel was flung open, and heavy footsteps came thumping down the passage. There was a bash on my door, and this young officer walked in, saluted me, and gave his name.

'I believe you have an officer here called So-and-So?' he said. 'I want a word with him.'

'You'll find him in the third office down the passage,' I replied.

Out he went, and straight into this other officer without even knocking. Then I heard a startled cry, the sound of two crashing blows, and the clatter of furniture going for six. I waited until I heard the front door slam to, and went along to see what had happened. There the gossip lay on his back on the floor, clutching his nose, with blood spurting between his fingers. I picked him up, dusted him down, and rather unsympathetically remarked that he had got what he deserved, and hauled him off to his quarters. As I was packing ice round his nose, which was really rather mangled, I was also worried that he would be so upset by the damage to his treasured good looks that he would want to lay a complaint against the young actress's husband. In the end, I more or less ordered him not to take the matter further, because it would have inevitably led to a court martial, and it seemed far more sensible to let the matter rest.

The officer stayed in his room for the rest of the day, but the next morning, when I heard him go into his office, I went down to see how he was. His nose was still pretty swollen, but he assured me that he was fine.

'I think you should go to hospital, because your nose is obviously broken. You can always say you had an accident in your car,' I suggested.

He shook his head.

'I don't think I shall have anything done to it,' he said. And then, turning his face sharply into profile, he added archly: 'As a matter of fact, I rather like the new shape it has now. . . .'

When I was finally demobbed in 1946, I must say I heaved a huge sigh of relief. Trying to run ENSA in India and the Far East might not have been as rugged and dangerous as fighting Japanese troops in the jungle, but there were times when it stretched the limits of sanity. After such an experience, even the prospect of being out of work in London seemed like a glimpse of paradise.

# SIX

The more I look back on my life, the more I realise how luck has played a major part in it. There is no doubt that in the acting business—as, probably in most others, too—without luck even a talented person can spend a great deal of his time sitting about with nothing happening at all.

During my last few weeks in India I spent many hours contemplating my future. What could an actor hope for in post-war London? I feared that while I had been shunting concert parties all over India and Burma, other younger actors, and indeed some of my contemporaries who had been unable to join the forces, would have filled the roles in the theatre that I might otherwise have been offered. Perhaps managements would have forgotten all about me? After all, I had been out of circulation for five years.

Perhaps I should go into the management of seaside shows instead of acting myself? God knows, I had enough experience of handling pier-end artistes! Certainly, the delight at the prospect of returning home was tempered with some nagging doubts about the future.

Shortly after the end of the war, I had to return briefly to London to see Basil Dean, who was in charge of ENSA, about policy now that the fighting was over. Understandably, all the touring companies out in the East wanted to come back, although thousands of troops were still out there, and more were joining them. Morale in the services was very low for they were also thinking about being demobbed, and resuming their civilian lives and careers.

It was wonderful to be back in London after nearly five years away, and although I was shocked by the extent of the bombing,

81

it was a tonic to see old friends, among them Alec Clunes, who was then running the Arts Theatre Club in London. He told me that the British Council had decided to set up a repertory company with a classical and semi-classical repertoire to tour, not only the major cities of Europe, but also the small towns and troop centres. Would I be interested in joining them after I had been demobilised? I said 'Yes' without a second thought.

All too quickly my time in England was up and I had to resume. As I was in charge of entertainment, for the whole of South East Asia Command, I spent my final months of duty travelling through India, Burma, Malaya and Ceylon.

In the meantime, Doreen had come back to London to resume her career as an actress, and had taken a small flat in Bedford Street, behind the Adelphi stage door.

On my return to be demobilised, she came to meet me at Euston—the troopship had docked at Liverpool—and we had a celebration. During the next few days we dined with Alec Clunes and he suggested that, as a stop-gap before the British Council tour, I should play King Magnus in Shaw's *Applecart*. I was delighted, for Magnus is without question one of the finest parts in British drama, but it is very long. One single speech that Magnus makes lasts for about nine minutes, and I hadn't learnt a role for six years. Could I accept the challenge that this represented?

Most of my friends thought I was quite mad to take on such a part for my return to the stage, but I thought that I might as well have a go, since I had nothing else to do with my time before the start of the British Council tour.

This was doubly welcome to me, for on my return the first letter I received was from the Inland Revenue with a large demand on my earnings at the Old Vic, five years earlier. I knew now I really was back in England! So far as the income tax people were concerned, I might never have left.

As events turned out, playing King Magnus was one of the best decisions of my career. The play was phenomenally well received, but, even more important, it gave me the courage and confidence to go ahead with the tour of Europe.

82

We opened in Prague. This was almost two years before the Communists took over, and although the Russians were there in considerable force, the city was swarming with Czechoslovakian freedom fighters and allied forces. Whatever menacing rumbles there must have been below the surface, these were not apparent in the way that our first presentation of *Othello* was received.

I shall never forget that audience. During the curtain calls they ran down to the orchestra pit of the Villariitskya Theatre and hurled huge bunches of flowers on to the stage in their way of thanking us all. It was an incredibly moving experience.

After years of brutal oppression under the Nazis, we must have represented a return of peace and hope for better times ahead. But how many people in that audience were so soon to see their dreams crushed by another oppressor?

Dee and I often ran into people during our travels in later years who had escaped from Prague to live in other parts of Europe, and who still remembered this performance—just as I did.

From Prague we went on to Austria, Holland and Belgium, and then the long leg down to the South of France to play in the Casino Theatre in Nice. This last was a rather weird experience, because the intervals were deliberately long, to give the audience a chance to break off and play the tables. It rather depended on how well they did as to whether or not they returned to see the next act!

During the visit to the Riviera, I drove to Cap Ferrat to have lunch with Somerset Maugham and fell in love with the peace and beauty of the place—never imagining that, one day, Dee and I would build a house there ourselves.

Leaving behind the roulette wheels and chemin-de-fer tables, we moved on to Italy, staging plays in Rome, Milan and Trieste, and finally we travelled to Switzerland. It was a long and extensive tour, involving a huge caravan of transports: now, of course, airlines have telescoped distance, but then we had to go by road and rail. We took everything with us—costumes and full sets—because we were not merely putting on productions in a set of curtains. Although it cost the British Council a considerable

83

amount of money, in the end it worked out at about half the price of one bomber and the good-will value was beyond calculation.

One of the oddest places we played in was Trieste, which at that time was a kind of buffer city between Italy and Yugoslavia. The British, American, Italian and Yugoslav forces lived there in an enclave similar to Berlin, but for our productions the British forces were the hosts.

We opened, as we did in most cities, with *Othello*, in which I was playing the title role. Following the performance we were all invited to a reception held in the mess of the British Officer Commanding. I arrived later than the rest of the cast, because it took a long time to clean off my black make-up. I had been given a drink by a mess-waiter, and was standing around feeling a bit lost, when Fay Compton, who was with the company, beckoned me over and introduced me to a rather blustering brigadier.

After we shook hands he said: 'Were you in the piece tonight?'

'Yes, I was,' I admitted.

'What part did you play?' he asked.

I looked at Fay, who was struggling to keep a straight face.

'As a matter of fact, I was Othello.'

'Good Heavens,' he said. And then he bellowed across the room, presumably to his wife: 'Muriel, come over here! I want you to meet this fella. He's the one who played the Zulu type.'

When we returned to London, wondering what we were going to do next, we were told that the H. M. Tennent organisation, which ran the Queens, Globe and Piccadilly Theatres, wanted us to do a short season of *Othello* and Shaw's *Candida* at the Piccadilly. This turned out to be very successful for me, although at the time I don't think I fully realised how important it was. While I was playing Othello a friend of mine, Bill O'Bryen, came to see the production. He had returned from the Army, was now the right-hand man of Sir Alexander Korda, one of the greatest film-makers in the country.

Bill managed to persuade Alex to come to the theatre—which he rarely visited—although I don't think that the great man saw my performance right through. I suppose I must have made a reasonable impression on him, though, because about ten days later I was summoned to meet him at the office of London Films at 146 Piccadilly, on the corner of Park Lane near Apsley House.

Korda told me that he thought I should go into films, and to back his words with action, offered me a three-year contract that guaranteed me £5,000 in the first year, £7,000 in the second and £10,000 in the third. Of course, many people earned much more in films, but, since I had come out of the army without any savings whatever only months before, I was in no mood to argue, and a further most important consideration was that now I could afford to marry Doreen and buy a home.

To be honest, I was astonished to receive the offer. I had made a number of moderate films before the war, and I had been told with brutal frankness that I had absolutely the wrong-shaped face for the screen. On top of this, I did still occasionally suffer from camera nerves that brought on a nervous twitch. But, as events turned out, I had no need for any qualms. Eight years later I was voted the number one box office draw of 1954. I was even credited with irresistible sex appeal, which is another quality I had not imagined I possessed. One journalist wrote in the old *Sunday Graphic*: 'Women fall like a ton of bricks for the strong, silent charm of actor Jack Hawkins. They have made him the biggest romantic idol in British films since the heyday of James Mason.'

It was encouraging to learn all this, but I remember explaining to someone around that time, who was questioning me enviously about romance on the screen, that all was not as it might seem. It is not always easy to get up at six and, after a long winter drive in the dark and a session in make-up, arrive on the set at a quarter to nine, be introduced to your co-star and go straight into a clinch.

Actually, this happened fairly rarely. The only woman I remember kissing in such circumstances—and enjoying it—was Claudette Colbert. She has such a marvellous sense of humour that she also saw the funny side of the tradition in which film love scenes seem invariably to be shot as early as possible in the day.

The first film I made for Alex Korda was *Bonnie Prince Charlie*.

This was not a very good film, and although it was fun to make, it was beset with disaster from the outset. The original director, Robert Stevenson, had worked on the script for about eighteen months, and possessed a very clear idea of what he wanted to do, but after we had been shooting for about five weeks, insoluble differences emerged between him and Alex, and he left the set. For a short while Alex took over the direction himself, then he brought in my old friend, Anthony Kimmins, who had written *While Parents Sleep*. Anthony was a fine director, but his real forte was light comedy and farce.

So far as I was concerned, this was a very happy period. For one thing, during the course of the film, Doreen and I hurried out of the basement flat we had rented in Chelsea, off to the local Registry Office to get married. It was a wet Friday and we held our reception in a local pub, The Moore Arms. The publican, an old friend, had managed to secure a crate of champagne. That was certainly the best day's work I ever did.

David Niven was playing the title role of the Bonnie Prince— and we forged a close relationship which has lasted through the years. I don't think that David enjoyed making the film. It was, naturally, a costume piece, and he was much more accustomed to acting either in uniform or beautifully tailored suits.

I remember passing his caravan on the lot one morning just as he was coming out resplendent in velvet jabou, kilt with a great Royal Stewart Tartan sash, sporran, claymore, dirk and three-cornered hat. He spotted me, drew himself up, and said: 'Jack, tell me honestly, do I look a—prick?'

David was always conscious of the fact that he did not have a traditional acting background, for he had done very little work on the live stage, and here he was working almost entirely with stage actors. A lesser man might have become difficult and belligerent about this, particularly since David was a considerable film star in his own right. But instead he showed great humility, and a very real regard for even the most stick-in-the-mud old actors. He was certainly one of the easiest people I have ever worked with and I was delighted when we were both given parts in another

86

Korda film, *The Elusive Pimpernel.* He was the Pimpernel and, with the aid of a lot of padding, I was the Prince Regent. I fear I would not need that padding now!

This film took such a long time to make that Doreen had two children before it was finished. Our eldest son was born just as I started work, and our second as we finished. I doubt if any similar film would be allowed to go on so long in the making these days, but in that post-war, pre-television period, money seemed no object in film-making. There were literally hundreds of extras and scores of super-numeraries who appeared on the set every day.

One incident illustrates the spendthrift attitude that dominated the studios. In the film, there was a tiny sequence in which Margaret Leighton, who was playing David's wife, had to come down a corridor and spot him through a crack in a door playing cards with me and some other men. That was all there was to it.

We started rehearsing, and Margaret had just walked up to the chink in the door, when the director stopped everything, and asked us what we were going to do in the room. We said we would deal out cards.

'Ah, yes,' he said gravely. 'But what game are you going to play?'

One of us suggested whist.

'No, no,' he said. 'What was the most famous game played in Regency times?'

Of course, none of us knew. Eventually, some character in the research department of the studio remembered some long-for-gotten eighteenth-century card game, but naturally nobody knew how to play it. All filming was therefore stopped and a production man drove up to London to scour the gaming clubs to find an expert. By early afternoon this gentleman was brought to the studio, and we spent the rest of the evening being taught the rules, before being sent home.

The following morning we gathered round the card tables in our costumes and wigs. The director then walked in and said: 'The room's too empty.' More extras had to be hired. Once again everything stopped while the casting people were sent out to rope in extras, who then had to be fitted with their costumes and wigs. The rest of us just gave up, went to the pub, and eventually home.

On day three we arrived to find the card-room overflowing with coloured waiters, whores and ladies of the town. There was barely room to move. In the end it took four days to shoot the scene, and then it ended up on the cutting-room floor. This palaver must have cost thousands, and every penny thrown away.

The shooting schedule of the picture was extended so much that I was actually released half-way through to go to Morocco to make another film with Tyrone Power, called *The Black Rose*, a mediaeval adventure story. I played the part of a great English archer. This was a boring part, and the only thing that redeemed it was that I had to learn how to use a six-foot yew bow in a convincing way. In the end, I became quite proficient.

I don't know why I was cast for the role. It was a kind of Tony Curtis part—before the arrival of Tony Curtis. They even gave me a T.C. haircut, and I had to lose all the weight I had put on for Prinny. The assets were meeting Tyrone Power, who not only was a joy to work with, but became one of my closest friends— Dee and I were broken-hearted when he died—and working with Henry Hathaway, who taught me filming the tough way.

There was one scene when I was fighting off a Mongol attack, and I had to shoot over the camera in the general direction of a target that had been set up as a guide. The camera-crew certainly had no confidence in my ability to shoot straight, and when I stepped out in front of the camera, they were rather pointedly cowering under a makeshift shield of sheets of thick cardboard. I drew the bow and let fly and, to everyone's astonishment, including my own, the arrow landed in the centre of the target.

Henry Hathaway came up and said: 'God damn it, you hit it!'

'Naturally,' I replied with dignity. 'I have been practising extremely hard for the past six weeks.'

'O.K. But don't overdo it!'

Henry was, and still is, an extraordinary man. In those days I think he was probably the most feared, yet respected director in America, for he had a sharp tongue and fired people at the drop of a hat, with the result that we had a kind of shuttle-service of technicians coming out of Morocco. They lasted for an average of about three days.

After our first showdown we got along quite well, because I simply said: 'All right, get someone else to play the part. I'll go home, I could not give a damn.'

Years later, after my operation when I lost my voice, he went out of his way to help me get back into films. Beneath his harsh exterior, he concealed a kindly nature; but when we worked in this picture, he concealed it completely! What I did not know then was that during the filming of *The Black Rose* he was himself suffering from cancer, although he made a remarkable recovery.

One of the hazards of filming in the open air is the sound problem. Ty and I had a scene where we had to walk through a local village. 'Bluey' Hill, the Australian assistant director, had filled the village with Arabs, goats, donkeys, mules and chickens— and we set off to shoot the scene.

But every time the cameras started to turn, we were halted by some noisy interruption. Finally, after thirty attempts, just as we thought we had completed it satisfactorily, a dog started barking and a baby began to cry. Hathaway yelled at 'Bluey' Hill in his own inimitable way to control the extras better. Bluey walked up to the baby's mother and in his broad Australian accent said: 'Lady, please give the baby to the dog and then we can all go home!'

Ty had just married Linda Christian, and so they were nearly always in a close embrace; but happily—as I was without Dee— we made up a threesome for dinner and on the journey from Ouazzane to Marrakesh, a new location, we travelled in their car with Ty's male secretary. The rest of the unit had gone ahead by coach and trucks and we set off some hours behind them.

On the way, on an empty stretch of road, in wild and mountainous country, we ran into a tremendous storm. Rain poured down, lightning split the sky and we felt that we must be the last people left alive—a feeling reinforced by discovering that a bridge across the river had been swept away by the force of the torrent.

There was no turning back, for a tree had been uprooted behind us and blocked the road. So we sat with the rain driving on the car roof, and the river rising, wondering what we should do—what we COULD do.

Then I saw a face at the window in the rain. I opened the window. A man was standing outside. He explained to us he was a Russian who owned—of all things in that desolate place—a restaurant. We would be welcome to shelter there. We took him at his word and raced through the rain to a very rough-looking building, little better than a wooden shack. We dried out our clothes in front of a stove, and he said, very kindly, that he would prepare a meal for us. The restaurant seemed a crude place and this prospect did not fill us with enthusiasm, so I was astonished by the magnificent dinner that arrived. We started with caviare, went on to chicken Kiev and ended with baked Alaska, served with excellent wines. Afterwards, he asked whether anyone would like a liqueur and Linda demanded a creme de menthe frappé—which was the only drink the host couldn't produce!

Here we stayed for three days, living like peasants in wood huts with goatskin blankets on truckle beds and eating like kings—waited on by a genuine White Russian Prince. And nobody knew we were there! Finally, the bridge was repaired and we drove on. When Dee came out to visit us, we all went back to celebrate—and had the same meal. I am sure that this Russian's restaurant now has five stars. He deserves them.

By my third year with Korda I had made four major films, and I was beginning to yearn for the live stage again, so when I was offered the part of Mercutio in a New York production of *Romeo and Juliet*, with Olivia de Haviland as Juliet, I jumped at the chance.

At that time Olivia was a tremendous name in films, and the whole of the 150,000-dollar production was built around her. Oliver Messel was brought in to design the sets and costumes, and Peter Glenville directed. The problem was that while Olivia was an internationally acclaimed film actress, she had limited stage experience. She had appeared once at the Hollywood Bowl in *A Midsummer Night's Dream*. Peter had, therefore, to concentrate his efforts on her performance.

To complicate matters, Olivia was at that time married to an author who, for some reason, made it his job to protect Olivia from Press publicity. The result of his very efficient endeavours was that when we were ready to open, the American Press was just not interested. This obsessive protection also succeeded in working Olivia into a frightful state of nerves.

When we were trying out the play in Cleveland—we also played Detroit, Philadelphia and Boston before opening on Broadway—Olivia's husband came to my dressing-room, looking as though he were plotting the assassination of the President.

'Jack,' he said. 'I want you to know that the house is full and there are thirty-five people standing.'

'That's fine,' I said, for it was.

'But,' he added, 'don't tell Olivia. It will make her nervous.'

'Why on earth should it make her nervous?'

'She will think there are too many people out there,' he replied, with the weirdest logic I have ever heard offered to an actor.

I would be dishonest if I try to pretend that fame and stardom are not attractive, but looking back on my own childhood and the remarkable closeness of our family life, I realise now that the career which has given me so much, has also robbed me of the normal everyday experiences of a father in a less publicised and demanding career.

When I was being named as Britain's top box office draw, and one of the highest paid, there was another price to pay that cannot be quoted in currency; it was the fact that I was being denied the chance to share in my children's childhood.

I was often on location far away for weeks or months, when Dee would deputise for me at speech days and half-terms and at Guy Fawkes children's parties. Even if I were home I would leave a sleeping household at dawn to make my way to the film studios and long tedious hours in the make-up chair, on the set, and then return, often exhausted, at a time when the nursery was silent, as when I had left.

When one has so few opportunities to spend time with one's children, I fear that one must invariably spoil them. It may sound slightly absurd to say that it would have been nice to have had the chance to lose one's temper with one's children like any other normal father, but these things are part of parenthood. But, in spite of many pressures, it was possible to find time to experience something closer to family life than I had ever achieved with my first child, Susan.

Since I was in New York, I decided that I should see Jessica, and, perhaps more important, Susan, my daughter by our marriage. Doreen knew what I had in mind and thought it a good idea. During the ten years since Jessica and I had parted, we had kept in touch by letter, but we had not met.

Jessica had established herself as a successful actress in America, particularly as a result of starring as Blanche with Marlon Brando in the stage production of Tennessee Williams' play, *A Streetcar Named Desire*, and she had married Hume Cronyn, a very good leading character actor, who came from a wealthy Canadian family. Anyway, having made the decision to see her, I telephoned Jessica and proposed we should meet.

'Of course,' she said at once.

'Let's meet and have a drink in the early evening at the 21 Club,' I suggested. The 21 was a favourite haunt of mine from prohibition days.

'Surely not the 21. That place is a hotbed of gossip,' she exclaimed.

'For God's sake, what is there to gossip about?' After all, we had been divorced for years; there was nothing between us but a shared past and one child. When I arrived and found a table I noticed that one of the other people there was the late Duke of Windsor. Somehow, he seemed a curiously apt link with the year when Jessica and I had married.

Shortly after this Jessica arrived. It was an odd experience seeing her, for she seemed to have changed very little. I felt almost as though I had seen her only the day before, and yet I felt a complete flatness at the meeting. There was no excitement, no resentment; just a feeling of there she was, and there she was gone.

I ordered drinks, and we chatted about this and that; my family, and hers, rather like acquaintances meeting casually in a bar. Eventually, I said that I would like to see Susan. She had been barely six when we had parted in London at the beginning of the war. Now she was sixteen, and naturally I was anxious to know what kind of a young girl she had grown into.

Jessica became oddly evasive.

'She's going back to school in two days' time,' she said.

'Well,' I said. 'You can send her round to my hotel tomorrow evening before she leaves, and I'll take her out to dinner.'

In the end this was agreed and I took her to the Algonquin. I think that this was the happiest evening I spent on that rather fraught stay in New York. But even so it was, inevitably, impossible to replace a gap of ten years in a single evening. I think that of all the effects of divorce, losing the chance to share in a child's growing and formative years is the saddest.

Susan was then very keen on a stage career and, although Jessica was not very enthusiastic, I wanted her to come to England to study at RADA, after she had completed her normal education. Finally, agreement was reached, but two years later, at about the time she would have been coming to London, Susan changed her mind and, instead of the stage, she decided to study child guidance at the University of California.

Considering the state of the acting profession now, this was undoubtedly a very wise choice. While she was at university she met a young engineering student, they fell in love, and married. Now they have children of their own, and live in a delightful home in Los Angeles; we all keep in touch.

When Dee arrived to see *Romeo and Juliet*, I asked her opinion of it.

'I shouldn't unpack too much,' she replied shortly.

I took her advice, which was fortunate, for this sumptuous production came off after six weeks, but nevertheless, so far as I was concerned, it was good to get the feel of a live audience again.

I remember our stay in New York with immense warmth; we had an apartment on 58th Street, and every night Dee would walk down to 44th Street to meet me after the performance. She walked alone—a thing that would be far from wise to do now, as everyone knows, including New Yorkers themselves, because of the risk of being mugged—something totally unthinkable and unheard of during our earlier visits.

When it became obvious that the play was going to collapse, I had a telephone call from London asking me whether I would read a script of a film that ABC at Elstree were planning to make. I think that almost any script would have been welcome at that particular moment; this one turned out to be *Angels One Five*, an RAF war film, in which I was being offered the part of a group captain. It was a good part, and a good script, and I jumped at the chance to return to films with such a story. This proved to be the part that set my feet on the road—I don't know whether I altogether care for the road—leading to a whole series of service character parts. Over the next few years, I played enough senior officers to stock the whole Ministry of Defence. I remember telling an interviewer for *Vogue* in 1956 that 'every time an army, navy or air force part comes up they throw it at me. There is nothing left now but the women's services!' So it seemed at the time, but to be accurate, I have played fewer Service types than John Mills, Trevor Howard and Richard Attenborough. But in the process I appeared to have acquired the reputation of being able to make better love to a battleship than to a woman! I submit that this is just not true, although I suspect that battleships may be a lot less trouble in the long run.

Before making *Angels One Five* I had been in uniform only once on the screen, in *State Secret*, with Douglas Fairbanks Jnr, in which I played a very sinister army character, who was also foreign minister of an Eastern European dictatorship. Doug played an American surgeon who was flown to the country to operate on the dying dictator. Unfortunately, the patient dies, and Doug is held incommunicado because the military government does not want the news to leak out and start a revolution. The story was of Doug escaping, with me pursuing him.

Only one thing marred the fun of making that film. For some rather obscure political reason it was decided that it would not be particularly tactful to use any language that might identify the country as being one of those behind the Iron Curtain, although it was pretty obvious it was just such a country that we had in mind. Instead, the production company decided to commission a remarkable lady linguist from London University to invent a language. She took her task very seriously, and created a completely usable language, grammatically impeccable, which had a kind of Serbo-Croat base, with Polish endings. It had only one disadvantage: for mere actors like us it was almost unspeakable. This splendid lady used to appear daily on the set to coach us in her precious language, and we were not allowed to make any mistakes.

I would say, for example, 'Niet van', and she would say, 'No. That's the wrong tense. It should be Niet vie.' This was all quite absurd, since nobody would be able to understand the language anyway, and was another example of a film company wasting money.

Doug had a marvellous time watching us struggling with this kind of Eastern European Esperanto, because with his part he was not expected to be able to speak it. Glynis Johns, who was playing a night club singer, did magnificently, and even had to sing a song in the language, but I am ashamed to say I never mastered it, and when I did grasp the pronunciation I forgot the words. Much of the action took place in my office where I was directing the chase after Doug, and I was able to overcome the problem by having my lines written in 'top secret' files, on the blotter on my desk, and on 'official bulletins' pinned around the wall telephone. Our efforts were not in vain, for we won an award at the Venice Film Festival in 1950.

*No Highway*, the film which followed, was a great leap forward in time and setting for me. It proved that I could put on a performance without wearing a wig or armour. It was adapted from

Nevil Shute's novel about a scientist trying to get an airliner grounded, because he believes that it is going to break up as a result of metal fatigue. Jimmy Stewart played the scientist with great brilliance, but the star I remember best in that film was Marlene Dietrich. She was so professional that I felt this was the first time that I had worked with a really great screen actress.

I was once sitting beside her during a lull between shots. She delved into her handbag and pulled out a small mirror, and all the time we were chatting she was looking into the mirror with a peculiar intensity. This struck me as an unusual display of vanity. Meanwhile, the French cameraman, one of the greatest cameramen of all time, George Beninalt, was supervising the lighting.

Suddenly, Marlene stopped our conversation and, pointing to the rack carrying the back lighting, said: 'George! Not number eighteen. Number seventeen. And a little more to the left.' She had been using the mirror to study the rigging of the lights which would show her to her best advantage. She is also, of course, a very fine actress, largely because she knows absolutely her own limitations; but within those limitations there is nobody to touch her.

It is very rare to make a film without learning something, and two years later, in 1952, I discovered what it was like to go through life with a truly crippling handicap. I believe that no experience is ever wasted; it is always stored in the banks of the mind, and this particular experience was later to be of tremendous help to me when I found myself a handicapped person. The film was *Mandy*, the story of a little girl who had been born deaf, was therefore dumb, and how she was taught to speak.

To start with, the proposition seemed rather vague. I was asked to meet the producer, Leslie Allman, and the film director, Alexander McKendrick, to talk over the story. There was no script, and so far as I could see, no real plans, but I liked the idea and the smell of it, and particularly the part of a headmaster of a school for the deaf and dumb, which I was being asked to play.

On the evening after the meeting, I was having a drink with some friends, and they asked what I was going to do next, and

96

I told them I had accepted a part in an, as yet, unscripted, unplanned film.

'You must be mad to take on something without even seeing the script,' they said. But, as it turned out, *Mandy* resulted in my getting the part of Captain Ericson in *The Cruel Sea*.

*Mandy* was a remarkable and moving experience, because most of it was shot on location in a school for the deaf and dumb in Manchester. I was overwhelmed with admiration for the staff. I had never met such dedicated people before, and what was so impressive was their patience and complete detachment from any sign of irritation; there was no question that these little children could be extremely irritating in their desperate need to communicate.

What was the most disturbing factor for me to begin with were the incoherent cries and shrieks the children made in their attempts to speak. Because they lived in a world of silence, for they had all been deaf since birth, they had no idea of the noise they were generating. However, after the first day or so, we became almost unaware of this world of total noise.

One factor in particular that helped to dispel any feelings of horror, or the simple desire to run away, was the unrestrained affection of the children. They gave themselves wholeheartedly to anyone who could be bothered with them. Their tremendous perseverance in trying to speak fascinated me, and I spent a lot of time trying to get them to lip-read me, or trying to communicate by gestures, with the result that three children took me over as their personal property.

Every morning, when I arrived for work, they would rush up to me, and would stay at my side for the day. The only problem was that when I was called away to do a scene, they wanted to come as well, and I literally had to peel them off me because they would climb all over me as though I were a tree.

I think it was because I became so involved with these children that I was able to play my part in the film with success. I never had any fears that my performance would be overwhelmed by little Mandy Miller, who was in the title role, or by the deaf and dumb

97

children we used as extras, although it is said that acting with a child or a dog is professional death to an adult actor.

The headmaster I was portraying was a passionate, even angry man, who was perpetually rubbing the bureaucrats up the wrong way, but for no motive other than the well-being of his children. It is rare to find a part with such depth of character, and *Mandy* remains one of my favourite films.

I was able to cope with the part because this was a time when I was acutely conscious of the value of family life, a value which I regard as paramount in anyone's existence.

# SEVEN

*Mandy* was undoubtedly the turning point in my career as a film actor. The fact that it helped me to sort out priorities in my own philosophical attitude to life was privately useful, but professionally it was the lever that pushed me from comfortable success to stardom. This stemmed not so much from the film itself, but from the fact that it led directly to the starring role in *The Cruel Sea*.

We had returned from Manchester where we had spent weeks on location work on *Mandy*, and were putting together the studio scenes at Ealing. At lunchtime on the first day's shooting in the studios I walked out across the road to The Red Lion for a gin-and-tonic. As usual, the bar was packed with film actors and technicians. I was taking my first sip when at the other end of the room I saw Charles Frend, one of the film directors at Ealing. He gave me the thumbs-up sign, and when he eventually made his way to me through the crowd, he said: 'I have just seen the first rushes of *Mandy*, and they are bloody marvellous.'

Naturally, I was delighted and we talked for a while about the film, when he suddenly said: 'Have you read *The Cruel Sea*?' I hadn't, largely because it had only been published three weeks before, and I had been completely tied up with the film, learning my part.

'Drop into my office this afternoon and I'll give you a copy,' he said.

Later that day I collected the book, and when I got home after the day's filming I sat down and read it from cover to cover. I thought it was brilliant. A couple of days later, Charlie sought me out and asked me what I thought of the book. I told him it was quite superb.

99

'That's good,' he said. 'Because you are going to play Ericson. It's all arranged. You are playing the part.'

And that is exactly how I got into the film, but I think my reception at the first night of *Mandy* must have confirmed the faith of the producer Sir Michael Balcon in my ability to handle the role.

I knew this film was a success because at the première we had a standing ovation and the warmth of the audience was unmistakable. So far as I personally was concerned, the really big surprise came when Dee and I, and with Bill O'Bryen and his wife Elizabeth Allan, came down the stairs into the foyer and a crowd of people waiting there instantly began to clap. I looked around to see who they were applauding—and realised with astonishment that they were clapping me. This was an overwhelming moment, which I can never forget.

Rather as in the case of *Mandy*, when I read the novel of *The Cruel Sea*, no script had been written, and no real plans had been made for the film. All that had happened was that the studios had bought the film rights of the book.

I filled in the time between the end of *Mandy* and the start of shooting *The Cruel Sea* making *The Planter's Wife*, with Claudette Colbert and Anthony Steel. I played a rugged character, a rubber planter in Malaya, who refused to be intimidated by the communist guerillas. It was full of action in the depths of the Malayan jungle, although I have to admit that we did not leave Pinewood Studios for one single day. All the outside work was done with that rather cheating technique of back projection, by which the action is played out against a screen showing moving pictures of locations (that were not even in Malaya, but in Ceylon). What made it all the more absurd was the fact that we were filming in the middle of winter, and dressed only in bush shirt and shorts I was permanently frozen.

I remember one scene very well. Claudette and I were sitting on the veranda of our bungalow having drinks and talking about the troubles. All around us were the sounds of the jungle—crickets whirring, frogs croaking and monkeys squealing. Above our heads a curtain, known as a punkah in the East, was being pulled to and fro to create a breeze, while we lounged in bamboo chairs, apparently in tropical heat but in fact frozen to the marrow.

The cameraman was lining up a close-up of Claudette, which was to be shot across me so that my forearm would be in the picture. He fiddled around for some time, then in an exasperated tone, said: 'It's no good. We've got to do something about this.'

'What's the matter?' the director called out. 'It's a very nice frame.'

'And the most outstanding thing in it,' the cameraman retorted, 'are the goosepimples on Jack's arm!'

Finally, they had to pack hot-water bottles under my tropical gear and wait until the goosepimples subsided.

*The Cruel Sea* was unlike any film I have made before or since. From the outset I had the feeling that it would either be a complete flop or a very great success, but either way it would never be mediocre. And watching it again on TV recently, I was proud of the way in which it had not dated; seeing it again also brought back so many memories.

All of us in the film were sure that we were making something quite unusual, and a long way removed from the Errol Flynn-taking-Burma-single-handed syndrome. This was the period of some very indifferent American war movies, whereas *The Cruel Sea* contained no false heroics. That is why we all felt that we were making a genuine example of the way in which a group of men went to war.

It had to be genuine; it could not be recreated in a plasterboard replica of a Navy fighting ship. In fact, the greatest problem was trying to find a corvette to star in the film. Corvettes were about the smallest escort vessels in the Navy, but they had done fantastic work in protecting convoys crossing the Atlantic, and across the North Sea to Russia. Quite small, about 1,200 tons, they were beastly little ships to sail in because they bounced around like corks, a fact I was to experience to my acute discomfort.

At the time the film was being planned, there were no corvettes in service with the Royal Navy, so we could not borrow one.

The Irish Navy maintained a couple, but at that particular moment relationships between Britain and Ireland were not particularly friendly, a situation that unfortunately seems to crop up from time to time. Rather cautious approaches were made to the Irish Government, and negotiations had actually begun, when the studio heard that there was a corvette in existence that had been loaned to the Greek Navy towards the end of the war. It had recently been handed back and was docked at Malta, waiting to be towed back to England to be broken up.

She was a Flower Class corvette called *The Coreopsis*, and from all accounts ideal for the role of the *Compass Rose*.

Captain Jackie Broome, one of the most experienced escort captains in the Navy, was engaged as technical adviser on the film, and he flew to Malta to inspect the vessel. He cabled back to say that he thought the corvette could be put into some kind of order, and after a few repairs somehow managed to sail her back to Plymouth where most of the filming was to take place. I remember meeting him on the day he got back and asking him how the ship was.

'We shall get her going all right, but God, what a state she's in. I can only tell you that when those Greek sailors went to the heads they must have turned cartwheels,' he said.

Jackie Broome is a splendid character, with all the bluff eccentricity that one associates with traditional naval types. Although he had retired from the Navy when he joined us, once he got his hands on the *Compass Rose* I think he convinced himself he was back in the service. For the duration of the film we took on a crew of Merchant Navy lads, but so far as Jackie was concerned they were naval ratings, and he treated them to the full blast of service discipline. Any man who got sloshed in the evening, and that was not an uncommon occurrence, would be wheeled into Jackie's office by his first lieutenant, and given the most tremendous dressing down. Naturally enough, this did not go down too well with the civilian sailors, and we almost had a mutiny before shooting a foot of film.

As far as seamanship was concerned, Jackie Broome could not

be faulted. He sailed—or drove—that corvette in the Channel and round Plymouth Sound as though it were a mini-car. Indeed, I think that much of the credit for the success of the film is due to his skill.

While I would stand on the compass platform scanning the horizon with war-weary eyes, Jackie would be crouched on a stool at my feet peering through a tiny hole in the bridgework, whispering navigating instructions down a voice-pipe, while I repeated them down my voice-pipe.

This all worked beautifully until one ghastly day, which we had spent filming out in the Channel. We were returning to base about mid-afternoon, when it was suddenly decided to shoot a sequence of the ship coming into the tideway basin at full speed. This delighted Jackie, who seemed to enjoy treating the corvette like a power-boat.

We had a pilot on board, as we always did when we came into the Sound, and we stood off waiting for the signal. Nothing came through and eventually the signalman came to the compass platform and said that the radio had broken down. A few minutes later, we spotted a figure waving frantically from the breakwater of the tideway basin, and we assumed that this was 'the off'. So it was full-speed ahead as we sliced through the Sound and right up to the entrance of the basin, only to see one of the assistant directors gesticulating madly and screaming: 'Go back! Go back!'

Although a corvette is a small craft, you can't stop her dead in her tracks, so we shot into the basin like an arrow to find it already packed with shipping. Jackie leapt up off his stool, and I retreated to the back of the compass platform. Somehow or other he executed a fantastic turn and whipped out into the Sound again.

The pilot let out a gasp of sheer relief, and turning to Jackie, he said from the depths of his heart: 'Captain Broome, I have seen some sailing in my time, but that was the finest yet.'

Jackie was almost purring with delight, his blood was up and he was thoroughly enjoying himself. Once again, we hung around in the Sound for about half an hour, during which time the radio was coaxed back to life, and we were eventually ordered to make the run again. The pilot didn't exactly say, 'I wouldn't do it if I were you,' but he did mention pointedly that the tide race was getting up a bit.

Again, I took up my commanding position on the compass platform, and once again we zoomed off for the basin, but this time with added impetus as the tide was also carrying us along. As we flashed past the breakwater, I saw moored alongside the quay, and almost exactly in our path, a beautiful destroyer, the *Camperdown*, which had just come from a refit, and was in the most superb condition. It is hard to describe the sense of impotence that swept over me as we bore down on this lovely craft, and with a frightful rending sound raked our anchor fluke along her side before coming to a standstill.

There was a terrible silence. No panic, no shouting, nothing at all, except the appearance of dozens of characters at the side of the destroyer, gazing down incredulously at our bloody little corvette.

I started to make rather desperate gestures to indicate that it was nothing to do with me, but that did nothing to deflect those rows of contemptuous and withering eyes. Finally I plucked up the courage to take a look at the hideous jagged scar that we had marked on to the destroyer. As I looked, a porthole opened and a sailor with blazing red hair and a face to match, who had obviously been woken from a very deep sleep, pushed his head out, looked this way and that, caught sight of me, and with heavy irony asked: 'Who's driving your bloody wagon then? Errol Flynn?'

That little knock cost the film company's insurance company £10,000.

One of Jackie's greatest joys was sending signals to passing Navy ships. The Navy has always had a great tradition of Aldis lamp and knowing that, as a civilian, he was beyond the reach of naval discipline, he never lost an opportunity to pass saucy remarks.

At the time we were filming, the USS *Missouri*, always known as the 'Mighty Mo', the largest battleship in the world, arrived at

Plymouth on a goodwill visit. She was the talk of the town for days. Even our activities paled into insignificance.

One evening we were returning to our mooring after a day's shooting, and were just chugging past the Mighty Mo when there was a great flashing of an Aldis lamp with the message: 'What ship are you?'

To this Jackie replied: 'We are *Compass Rose* sailing the cruel sea. What ship are you?'

Needless to say, we received no reply.

When I was, in the film, given command of the frigate, *Porchester Castle*, it was glorious mid-summer weather, quite perfect for cruising in the Channel, but we were supposed to be in the North Sea, in the middle of winter. The front half of the frigate, including the first half of the bridge, had therefore to be artificially iced-up. The art department and the plasterers got to work, and draped the superstructure and guns with plaster icicles, ice and frost, all covered with that glitter dust that is used to decorate Christmas trees. By the time they had finished, I felt it was like taking a floating wedding-cake to sea.

On top of this decoration, we had to dress suitably for the Arctic Circle in boots, heavy sweaters and duffle coats and, dripping with sweat, we would make for the open sea, weaving our way through flocks of sailing yachts and pleasure boats.

After the *Compass Rose* was 'sunk' in the film, she left the company and made her final trip to Newcastle to be broken up. This was a sad moment for all of us, because she had behaved beautifully for the film, although her finest pieces of dramatic expression proved extremely uncomfortable for all of us on board.

For many of the scenes it was necessary to find rough seas, which at the time of year we were filming were rare. About the only place we could guarantee the right effect was in the Plymouth Race, where about seven currents converge, and where the sea can be very crusty indeed. When the Race was really playing up, the *Compass Rose* used to behave like a corkscrew, and almost turn on her head, which was fine from the camera's point of view, but ghastly for the rest of us. I was supposed to look like a seasoned old sea-dog, but the fact is that I have always suffered from sea-sickness. Fortunately I never actually threw up, but I used to feel damned ill after these scenes.

I really have to thank Jackie Broome for providing the key to the technique of playing the part of Ericson. It was entirely by observing his absolute calm in any circumstances that I was able to produce a convincing portrayal of a good naval officer. In a way I regret that so many people remember my characterisation of Ericson as being an archetype of the stiff-upper-lip school of officers, because I am an emotional man, and I can do other things than sticking out my over-blown jaw.

I think the main flaw in my performance of Othello in 1947 was that I felt too emotionally about the character. I used to come out in floods of tears at the drop of a hat and, unlike some actors who have to have sprays discharged into their eyes to get them to cry, I have always been able to produce tears to order with no difficulty at all.

There was one incident in *The Cruel Sea* which affected me very deeply. This was when we had been escorting a convoy which was disastrously cut up by U-boats, with a loss of about seventy per cent of the merchant vessels. At the height of the destruction, the *Compass Rose* picks up an asdic signal that there is a submarine directly below, and I have to make the dreadful decision to plough through the group of British sailors struggling in the sea, dropping depth charges among them.

Eventually, the decimated convoy reaches Gibraltar, and Ericson goes ashore and gets completely stoned. This was followed by a very brief scene back on board when his Number One, Lockhart, who was played by Donald Sinden, comes up to him at the rail and asks if he is all right. Ericson says he is far from all right, and launches into a diatribe justifying the terrible decision he had to take.

It was an extremely emotional scene, and the more I thought about the situation the more upset I became, and the tears just poured down my face. When we had finished everyone said the scene had come off marvellously, but a couple of days later Mick Balcon came on the set looking a little distracted, and went into a huddle with the director, Charles Frend. Eventually, they both came over to me.

'I have just seen the scene on the deck cut together,' said Mick. 'And I think it's a little too emotional. I would like you to do it again.'

So a few days later we re-shot the sequence, and this time I kept my feelings under control and played it absolutely dry. When we had finished Mick came over and said: 'That's just right.'

A couple more days passed, and there was another discussion in the corner of the set, and once more Mick and Charles approached me. They had seen the new version cut together, and they thought it was not quite emotional enough. What they wanted was a compromise between the two versions we had done. This time I shed one tear in the place of two, and everybody seemed happy. Indeed, after the rushes were screened the following day I was told that the scene was now 'dead right'.

In fact, when the film was finally completed, they used the first version!

Working with the frigate was tremendous fun, largely because we were loaned a Royal Navy crew, who became very involved in the filming. I think they all secretly hoped that they might be spotted for stardom, because we never had any lack of volunteers to fill in as extras.

We had a couple of days when we were shooting the sinking of a U-Boat and needed men to act as the crew of the submarine we rescued. This was a pretty unenviable role, for they had to be smeared with oil and dropped over the side. They then had to swim around in oily water before being hauled back on board in nets. Yet they were all mad keen to get in on the act.

On the first day I was walking along the gangway when a stoker emerged from the bowels of the ship and said: 'Mr Hawkins. Permission to speak.'

'Of course,' I replied. 'What is it?'

'It's about all these blokes playing in this rescue scene. Well, sir, it's not fair, because down in the engine room we haven't been offered a chance to take part.'

'I suppose you know that it means being covered in oil, chucked in the sea and pulled out again?'

'Yes,' he said. 'But we would like our chance along with the rest.'

So I had to go to the captain and explain that he had a potential mutiny on his hands. In the end, we ran a ballot to select the men to act as extras.

The success of *The Cruel Sea* is now, of course, cinema history, and from a personal point of view I would be falsely modest if I did not admit that I enjoyed the experience of becoming a big star; not only the large fees and the good parts that came my way as a result, but also recognition in the street by strangers who had enjoyed my performances.

But the memento I treasure most is a copy of *The Cruel Sea* that Nicholas Monsarrat sent to me with this inscription on the flyleaf: 'To Lieutenant Commander and Mrs G. E. Ericson (masquerading as Mr & Mrs Hawkins) with salutations and all the thanks in the world.'

# EIGHT

Since *The Cruel Sea* I have never been out of work and, even now, despite the handicap of my strange style of speech, I am still making films although, obviously, major roles are now denied me.

Some of the films have become famous in their own right, like *The Bridge on the River Kwai*, *Lawrence of Arabia*, *Gideon's Day* and *Lord Jim*. Others, like *Land of the Pharaohs* and *Rampage*, are probably best forgotten. But however badly films may turn out in the end, they all have their moments of charm.

Perhaps surprisingly, it took some years before I was invited to Hollywood although I had made a number of films for American companies, but always on location. I think that no actor should take Hollywood too seriously, but at the same time it would be wrong to underestimate its professionalism. Really, Hollywood is a caricature of itself, and in particular this is true of the front-office types at the studios. Their enthusiasm towards you is measured precisely to match the success of your last film.

Fortunately, when I went there to make *The Spinster* with Shirley MacLaine I was a big box-office draw and was treated as a valuable property, to be handled with care. But on the studio floor that atmosphere of graded sycophancy was completely missing. No other film centre can touch Hollywood crews for their dedication.

In England in those days one seemed to be surrounded by young boys covered with zip-fasteners who said they wanted you in at seven-thirty in the morning, and then you would end up sitting around on your backside until four in the afternoon. But in Hollywood one would find that assistant cameramen and focus-pullers would be quite elderly men who had spent a lifetime specialising in their field, and being very well paid for it.

Everyone knew their job backwards, and exactly what they wanted; consequently, there was no unnecessary time-wasting.

I think I was particularly lucky in being introduced to Hollywood filming by Shirley MacLaine. She is a very bright, honest person, although absolutely scatty in a delightful way. One thing she could never stand was any hint of pompousness or hypocrisy. As soon as she suspected this in a person she would send them up quite unmercifully.

I was lionised by Hollywood society, particularly while I was making *Five Finger Exercise* with Rosalind Russell, for she is one of the reigning queens of Hollywood. I arranged for the studio to install me in the Beverly Hills Hotel, still my favourite hotel in the world, in an extremely comfortable suite.

I have always been particularly fortunate in the American actors with whom I have filmed, such as Jimmy Stewart and Bob Mitchum. Bob and I made a film together called *Rampage*. This was supposed to be set in Malaya, although in fact we shot most of it in Hawaii. But for Bob, it would have been a grisly experience.

His attitude to acting is that it is a game to be enjoyed, usually on his own terms, which normally meant driving the production company to the verge of insanity. He had a running gag about losing his script, which never failed to produce a flutter of anxiety. He would come loping on to the set with an air of vagueness just before shooting was about to start.

'Am I supposed to be here?' he would drawl. 'I don't know what I'm meant to do, and I've lost my script.'

Immediately there would be a frantic flurry as production aides rushed around searching for a spare script, while Bob lounged sleepily in his chair. Eventually, a script would be produced and he would flip through it and say: 'Oh, yes. NOW I see what I have to do.' Then he would get up and play the scene absolutely word perfect down to the last comma and dot.

He is a superbly professional actor, but for some reason he tries to disguise this. There must also have been times when the production people doubted whether he would ever turn up for work, because Bob liked his drink and had a great head for it. In Hawaii he discovered a shattering drink called a Maitai, which is an enormous cocktail made from pineapple juice and seven different types of rum, all mixed together in a huge jar. I have known him have seven of these before dinner, which works out at about forty-nine tots of rum, and yet stay as cool as a cucumber. After three, I could just about make it to my bed.

Another superb man to act with is William Holden. Bill and I were in *The Bridge on the River Kwai*. I played the part of a former university don who was running a commando training school, and Bill was my rather unwilling partner in the attack on the bridge that the Japanese had forced allied prisoners-of-war to build. While we were doing location shots and living in a camp close to the bridge itself I discovered that Bill had an absolute obsession about fireworks. I suspect this is because in America one is not allowed to let off fireworks in a garden, and displays are always big public affairs.

One evening after shooting he and I walked down to the little village a short way from the camp to buy a few things from the store, which was like a jungle supermarket. I had just paid for some shaving soap when Bill pointed to a box of cardboard tubes on a shelf above the store-keeper's head.

'What are those?' he asked the Singhalese proprietor.

'Those,' he replied, 'are very fine, very great Roman candles.'

Bill's eyes lit up like fireworks at this intelligence, and before I realised what was happening he had bought the lot.

'You like fire-balloons?' the store-keeper inquired.

'Sure.'

The man then went into the back of the shop and came out with a huge bamboo globe covered with tissue-paper. This was about ten feet high, and had a little burner which fitted underneath it. This was added to the collection, and we carted the lot back to the camp.

That night, Bill organised the first of a series of spectacular firework displays. After we had set off the Roman candles, the fire-balloon was launched, blazed across the sky and came down about two miles away by the river.

The next evening, Bill said 'Come down to the village. I'm going to buy some more fireworks.'

This time he bought up all the Roman candles he could find, but he couldn't get a fire-balloon because the store-keeper had run out of tissue paper. Bill was disappointed at this, but I remembered that I had about three weeks' supply of the air-mail edition of *The Times*, which is printed on very flimsy, light-weight paper. The next evening we were back in the village with a large bundle of old copies of *The Times*, and found that the paper was perfect for fire-balloons. By now the local firework makers were practically on overtime trying to keep pace with Bill's insatiable appetite for pyrotechnics.

About this time Sam Spiegel, the producer, who had been away on a business trip, returned to the location, and Bill decided to lay on a display for him, culminating in the launching of his latest and biggest fire-balloon. It soared into the sky magnificently, and then started to drift towards the Bridge on the River Kwai, which had been built at a cost of thousands of dollars.

Sam nearly went mad when he saw there was a good chance that his precious bridge could be burnt down before he had the chance to blow it up! With a cry of despair he jumped into his jeep and went bouncing down the jungle tracks in hot pursuit, leaving the wicked Holden literally dancing with delight. Fortunately the balloon came down in the river. In fact it is amazing that the bridge ever did get blown up at all, or at least while the cameras were actually turning, because the first attempt was a near disaster.

The bridge had to be blown up as a train was travelling across it. Seven cameras were set up in hides, with slit trenches next to them in which the crews could shelter from the actual explosion.

As soon as the safety lights went on, showing that the cameras were rolling, a signal was given to the train driver to start up in a cutting about thirty yards from the first span. Just before the train reached the bridge the driver had to jump clear, leaving the engine to carry on to the centre of the bridge where the explosion would take place.

All the local tribesmen had been cleared out of the area for safety, and Sam invited about half the Government of Ceylon and their wives and families to watch the display from a quarter of a mile downstream.

I took Dee with Bill's wife, Ardis, and Sam's wife, Betty, to see the fun. We were all old film hands, and knew perfectly well that there would be some kind of delay, so we were well armed with sandwiches, and two large Thermos flasks of Bloody Marys. Then we picked a shady spot with a good view and settled down to enjoy ourselves.

We waited and waited and of course nothing happened, so we had almost finished the sandwiches and were unscrewing the second flask when the signal sounded for action. The train steamed into view at what seemed an excessive speed, shot across the bridge, disappeared into a cutting on the other side, and a second or so later there was a hideous crunch, followed by a crash. We finished up the Bloody Marys, because there was really nothing better to do, and concluded that something very nasty had happened. The ghastly point seemed to be that the bridge hadn't actually blown up.

What had happened was that one of the camera crews had jumped into their slit trench without pressing the button giving the all-clear for the detonation, but at the same time somebody at the control centre had given the train the go-ahead and the driver, in jumping clear, had hit the throttle with his arm, so that the train roared over the bridge and smack into a huge generator truck parked in the cutting.

As a result of the impact the train jumped the lines but, by the grace of God, came to rest on the edge of a 400-foot drop on to a road. Fortunately, nobody detonated the charge, because it had taken a Swedish engineering company nine months to build the bridge.

I think the saddest man that day, apart from Sam Spiegel, was the explosives expert from ICI who had spent hours wallowing around in the river planting the plastic explosive charges—particularly as he had to dive back to retrieve them, because plastic

113

explosives tend to become unstable if they are submerged in water.

On reflection, there was a second very sad man—Bill Holden, who was marooned on the other side of the river. After this shambles he swam the river, shore to shore, simply to have a Bloody Mary—only to discover we had drunk them all!

Meanwhile, the locomotive had to be man- and elephant-handled back on to the track, the locals had to be located and warned to continue staying clear of the area, and then at precisely ten o'clock the following day, as the train reached the centre of the bridge, everything went up. It was a magnificent achievement, and even satisfied Bill Holden's explosive genius.

I loved working on this film because it was almost entirely shot in Ceylon, which is a country to which I am devoted. In fact, it was largely because of me that this location was chosen. When we were discussing the film in London there was a great deal of concern expressed about how we were going to get supplies and technicians into the jungles of Burma where the story is set.

During the war, Dee and I had spent a good deal of time in Ceylon, and I had used any excuse I could think of to make a trip to the island, for it was a total and refreshing change from India. It was still under the benign influence of the British, particularly the British Navy, and it always seemed comfortable and welcoming.

I remembered a part of the country about thirty miles from Colombo that fitted exactly the terrain described in the story of *The Bridge on the River Kwai*, and told Sam Spiegel about it. He sent people out to take a look, and decided to make the film there.

Perhaps I also helped Alec Guinness to make the decision to play the British colonel who becomes obsessed by the building of the bridge, and it was just as well that I was able to jog him into the part, because his brilliant performance really made the film.

We had worked together as young actors in the theatre with John Gielgud. More recently, we had filmed *The Prisoner* together, and I found this one of my most rewarding acting experiences—if not financially—but then Alec and I were amateurs on the production side of the business, but we both loved to act.

After I decided to accept the part in the Kwai film that had been offered to me, I had a telephone call from Alec.

'Jack,' he asked, 'are you really going to do this bridge thing in Ceylon?'

'Yes, all things being equal, I am. I think it's a splendid story, and you will be terrific in the part they want you to play.'

'I don't know what to think, Jack,' he went on. 'I'm not at all sure.'

Two days later, he rang me again.

'Are you really sure you're going to do it?'

'Yes,' I said. 'Don't worry.'

'Well, if you're prepared to do it, I'll do it, too.'

In the evenings, when we had finished work, Alec used to take a fishing rod down to a muddy river—the Kwai in the film—and spent hours casting away like mad, with a landing net on hand for the catch that never materialised. There was one very exciting evening when his hook did get stuck into something, but after a long struggle it turned out to be only a rotten and submerged log. When he complained of his bad luck, I replied that he was fortunate not to have hooked a crocodile—which, in that river, far outnumbered the logs.

Alec finished his part of the film ahead of me, and on leaving gave me his rod and landing net. I was no more successful, and when I returned to England I gave the tackle to my eldest son, Nicky. I must say, he has been a lot more successful than either Alec or I had been.

Some months after we had finished shooting, Alec rang Dee and said he had seen the film run through, and told her in an astounded voice that it really was good, and everyone was excellent.

'In fact,' he said rather sheepishly, 'I think I'm quite good in it myself, too.' And, of course, he won an Oscar for his part.

Ironically enough, our joint lack of financial judgment was demonstrated once more, for we had accepted set fees while dear

Bill Holden, much more wisely, held out for a piece of the film, and deservedly made a fortune.

While making *The Bridge on the River Ku ai*, I think that some of my happiest off-duty hours were spent watching elephants as they worked on the building of the bridge They were mainly female elephants, and seemed to have some kind of trade union of their own, because about every four hours, just as though someone had blown a whistle, they would drop whatever they were carrying in their trunks and lumber into the river for a long swim and a soak, followed by a good feed. Nothing could persuade them to do otherwise.

There was one I particularly remember—a beautiful, intelligent, gentle creature. I watched her once carrying a huge teak log curled in her trunk and resting on her tusks. She had to get it into the river endwise, so she carefully positioned it on the bank, and started to push with her head, but it stuck fast. After a good deal of heaving, she straightened up and looked crossly at the log. You could almost hear her say: 'Bugger it.'

Then, slowly, she turned round, fitted her foot into the log, and with one tremendous shove sent it flying into the middle of the river.

We had many difficulties in making this picture, but sometimes film companies seem to make life complicated for themselves quite unnecessarily. For example, before making *Kwai*, I played the part of Pharaoh Khufu in a perfectly ridiculous film called *The Land of the Pharaohs*. We filmed it in Luxor, the Valley of the Kings and at Gizeh, where the Pyramids were built. In fact, the film was about the building of the Great Pyramid.

The problem was that in the film the Pyramids were supposed to be in the course of construction, but by 1955 they had a distinctly antique appearance, added to the fact that the marble that had clad them 5,000 years before had been looted by Napoleon's troops.

One morning I was sitting having a drink on the shaded balcony outside the hotel overlooking the Pyramids. Between sips, I noticed a gang of men crawling about the Great Pyramid in a cloud of dust. About lunchtime I wandered into the bar to find a very parched American special-effects man swilling down pints of iced beer. Between drinks, he told me that he and a gang of Egyptian workmen had been spending that morning sweeping the Pyramids.

'Did you ever hear anything so crazy?' he asked. I had to admit that I had not. On top of that, he had to rig canvas panels disguised to look like marble. Why Howard Hawkes, one of the old school of directors, went to so much trouble I will never know, because some of the lines we were expected to speak were unspeakable.

One of the reasons I had taken the part was that I had been told that the script was being written by William Faulkner. Frankly, I don't think that a single line that I uttered was written by so distinguished a writer, and indeed I later discovered that Faulkner had been hired to do the job, had received a huge fee, but somehow had got stuck in Paris. Other pens and typewriters had written the script. As a result, I spent a good deal of my time muttering and cursing over the frightful lines I was expected to utter. Howard overheard me once when I was worried about a key line in a particular scene.

'Don't worry,' he said reassuringly. 'I'll find you another. I have more used lines at my fingertips than anyone you know.'

He was quite honest about it. When he was short of dialogue, he would borrow lines from some old movie. I am quite sure that I ended up speaking words that Clark Gable had used in some quite different film.

In my desperation to make something of the part, I plodded round the Cairo museum studying the behaviour of Pharaohs depicted in the friezes. None of this, however, resulted in my being treated like a monarch by the film company, despite the myth that in the film world if you are playing a king you are treated like one, and if you play a pauper you are treated on a similar level.

There was a scene towards the end of the film when I was supposed to be dying. I was carried across the desert on a huge palanquin borne on the backs of slaves. As usual, there were the inevitable delays. I was draped in heavy robes, wearing a brass helmet and carrying my sceptre. While apparently thousands of extras were being organised into their places and told what to do, I was instructed to stay put.

It grew hotter and hotter, and a couple of British property men sitting on a truck just off-set were settling the dust by swigging big bottles of ice-cold beer. Every time they took a pull they raised their bottles to me gravely and said: 'Cheers.'

Eventually I could not stand it any longer, and I told them they were 'sons of bitches'. At this, one of them smiled sweetly and emptied half a bottle into the sand. I rather doubt whether any Pharaoh was treated quite like that!

# NINE

Being a film star, like winning the football pools, is something that many people dream about from time to time.

Fame, wealth and recognition are attractive assets to any life, but they do bring special problems. In the theatre, success means strains that in some cases have proved a tragic burden. One only has to remember Marilyn Monroe and Judy Garland to know that the stresses of stardom can become intolerable and finally unbearable.

I have always been fortunate in being able to treat the whole razmataz of stardom at worst with a kind of cynicism and at best with amusement. I would be less than honest, too, if I did not admit that I have enjoyed such fame as I have attracted. As I am rather gregarious by nature, recognition by the public has given me great personal pleasure, and I warm to the feeling of an audience and the spontaneous applause that greets a good performance.

But, as in most professions, when you reach the peak, you can find yourself perched on a pinnacle from which it is all too easy to fall. For some people this balancing act becomes such a torture that the only relief is in jumping off and, of course, there are plenty of people scrambling up towards your eyrie who are eager to give you a shove to send you on your way down.

I think what has protected me from moments of despair is the fact that I have always been secretly rather astonished that I reached the top in the first place. There have also been other reasons for my relative ease of mind.

First, I was brought up in the theatre, which imposed an almost military discipline on its players. It did not matter whether you were the humblest stage-hand, walk-on actor or the star of the piece, the play was the most important thing. There were some-times displays of emotion and arrogance, but these soon wilted under the abrasive tongues of men like Basil Dean.

This was certainly true of the British theatre, although I think that Hollywood has always had a rather callous attitude towards building or destroying its stars. But apart from the disciplined training I received from boyhood, I was fortunate in having a very stable childhood. My family, I am certain, was proud of me, but they never stuck me on a pedestal. They had their fair share of misfortune, which has always made me grateful for the success I have achieved.

During the slump of the 1930s, my father's public works con-tracting firm was one of the many victims. It tottered, and finally collapsed altogether, bringing down not only my father, but my brother, Tom, who had joined my father in the business. In the end, poor Tom, who is now dead, became the verger at St Michael's Church, Wood Green, where I had spent many happy years as a chorister.

Had I not been lucky enough to go on the stage, there is little doubt that I would have worked with my father and brother and been personally involved in the financial crash, which was a sobering thought. But, of all the influences that have shaped me, undoubtedly the most stabilising element in my life has been my own family—Dee and the children. Apart from being the perfect wife for me, Dee is an ideal actor's wife. Because she was on the stage herself, she fully understands and appreciates the pressures of the profession as well as the ordinary values of family life.

Very shortly after we were married, she decided that it would be unwise for both of us to attempt to follow acting careers—indeed this was one of the main reasons why my first marriage had come to grief. She wanted children, and also to make a home for me, and I must say she has achieved both ambitions superbly.

She is very calm and efficient, and in the early 1950s, when I started to make big money in films, there was no rush into extrava-gant displays of wealth. We continued to live in our flat in Chelsea

*Leslie H. Baker; Woman's Own*

1953—early days at Roehampton,
with Nick aged five (aloft) and Andy, two

At a Royal Première in November, 1954 at the Empire, Leicester Square.
Nick was to present the bouquet to the Queen

1955, when Nick was seven and fishing a great passion

As Major Warden in *The Bridge on the River Kwai* (1957)

*League of Gentlemen* (1960). At the back, camera-man Arthur Ibbetson, director Basil Dearden and myself. On the left, Terence Alexander, Norman Bird and Keiron Moore. On the right, Bryan Forbes, Roger Livesey and Richard Attenborough, and at the front Nigel Patrick

Receiving the *Ben-Hur*
award from the Duke of
Edinburgh in 1960

*Daily Herald*

The winter of 1962,
with Andrew (twelve),
Caroline (eight) and
Nick (thirteen)
*Sunday Pictorial*

The day I left London's University College Hospital,
10 February 1966

With Nick, working on a film in Africa (October, 1971)

With Dee at the première of *The Ruling Class* (1972)
of which I was a co-producer

until, with our growing family, we needed something larger with a garden where the children could play.

I was working very hard at the time, and so was largely unaware of the growing domestic chaos in Chelsea. Dee, however, was out every day secretly house-hunting.

She rang me one day at Pinewood.

'I've found a house,' she said. 'Do come straight home and have a look at it.' And then she added rather cautiously, 'It's a bit of a mess.'

That evening, we drove to Roehampton and pulled up at a solid family house that had been built in the 1930s. The garden was like a hayfield, and the house had that rather gloomy atmosphere of a building that has not been occupied for years.

I remember being rather scathing about its appearance, but in the end I agreed to buy. I had never fancied living so far out of central London, but at least this house was big enough for our family, and for more, and situated ideally for all the studios. It became the most lovely family home; the perfect foil to my more frenetic life as a film star.

This house at Roehampton was really the first major possession I bought out of the profits of stardom. In the years that followed, when I was being paid a lot of money for each film I made, I could have moved to bigger and grander houses. But when you create a home it adopts a character which is hard to abandon by moving away. Instead, we lived in Roehampton for eighteen years, before coming back to live in central London.

I suppose if I had been strictly practical I would have taken my family to Switzerland to escape the punitive taxes in Britain. But of all the countries in which I have lived and worked, none has ever equalled Britain in my eyes, and both Dee and I were determined that our children should have an English education. This is a decision I have never regretted. We do own a small corner of a foreign field, however—a house in the South of France, which I love dearly, and which will be the last thing I sell. This was also discovered by Dee while I was making a totally forgettable film in Nice for a Swiss company, in which I played

General Cornwallis busily losing the American colonies in the eighteenth century.

It was such a silly film that I decided I would not accept the part. But the more I backed down, the more money I was offered until the fee became so attractive I could resist no longer. This was genuinely the only bit of acting I have ever done solely for money, so maybe I deserved the discomfort of having to sit on a horse for hours every day while explosives were set off all around it to simulate a battle.

However, there were compensations. Each week, I would receive a cheque drawn on a Swiss bank. When the cheques reached a total of £30,000 I thought I had better do something about them, so I went to Barclays Bank in Nice and handed them over to the manager.

In the meantime, Dee had been exploring the countryside, and discovered a plot of land for sale on the sea at Cap Ferrat, which brought back memories of the day I had lunched there with Willie Maugham in 1946. This seemed an ideal investment.

The day before I finished the film, I went back to Barclays to draw out some money for the tips and presents which are traditionally expected by studio staff from the stars of films.

'Certainly,' said the bank manager. 'What travellers' cheques do you have?'

'What about all this money I've put into the bank?' I replied.

'Ah,' he said. 'You can't touch THAT money. It can't be moved or drawn out without special permission from the Bank of France. Any money banked by a foreigner goes into a special account.'

Certainly that was one way of helping France's balance of payments, but I was not so fond of the country that I wanted to solve its economic difficulties single-handed.

When I returned to London I made an appointment with an official at the Bank of England, who assured me there was nothing I could do about my frozen francs. After a while, I heard from France that I had been granted a stranger's account and so could use the money. But this was not to be so, because the Bank of England then said that if I did withdraw the money I must repatriate it all to England! I argued that I had earned the money in France, but to no effect.

In the end, instead of being able to pay for the land on the spot with the money I had earned in France, I had to bring it all back to Britain and sell the francs to a firm of foreign exchange brokers, then buy them back again with sterling. Finally I had to send them to France to pay for the land and the property, which Dee designed, and we proceeded to build.

This house, with its beautiful garden by the sea, has given the children, ourselves and our friends infinitely more pleasure and happiness than any amount of money could ever have provided.

# TEN

I have never been particularly concerned about personal possessions, although I am an enthusiastic collector of Staffordshire figures, and theatrical pictures, but, casual as I may be, I have never had quite such a disinterested attitude to my property as the Duchess of Medina-Celli.

This lady lent her exquisite fourteenth-century home, the Casa Paladuz in Seville, to Sam Spiegel for some of the location work for *Lawrence of Arabia*, in which I played General Allenby.

The building was said to be a copy of Pontius Pilate's palace in Jerusalem, and had been built from plans brought back from the Crusades. Whether this was true does not really matter, because it is quite superb in its own right. When I arrived there to do some scenes, I was horrified to see this beautiful palace and its contents being subjected to a barrage of film industry weapons, but far from being worried, the Duchess seemed thrilled to bits.

Fortunately, Sam, being a man of great taste—he owns one of the best collections of modern art in the United States—was more aware of the dangers than she appeared to be, and since we were filming on the upper floors, he had shored them up with great skill to prevent the weight of the cameras and equipment bringing down the ceiling.

Amazingly, no structural damage was done, but there was still a disaster of another kind. In the centre of the building was a magnificent courtyard, which had statues in each of its four corners. One of these was said to be priceless because it had been carved by Pheidias, the Carver of the Gods, the legendary sculptor of Periclean Athens. The other three statues were of Roman origin.

One morning, Peter O'Toole, who played Lawrence, and I

were drinking coffee on the veranda overlooking this courtyard, when I noticed a look of horror freeze on Peter's face. I followed his gaze and saw that a massive inch-thick cable was being hauled up through a window by a couple of technicians. It was draped over one of the Roman statues, and before we could shout a warning someone gave it a terrific tug, and a reinforced junction hammered the arm off the statue—a kind of instant Venus de Milo transformation.

A rather nasty hush fell over the courtyard, broken only by the scampering feet of the art director rushing to inspect the damage. Apart from being broken off, the arm had also broken in two parts as it hit the ground, although fortunately this was a very clean break.

The Duchess was not present at the time, but she arrived later with some friends to watch the filming. Before lunch, she invited Peter and me to have a glass of sherry. We were both feeling slightly sheepish and embarrassed, and said how sorry we were about the accident.

'It IS a pity, isn't it?' she agreed casually. 'But I am sure it can be repaired quite easily. And, after all, it WAS only Roman.'

I remember another day when she was showing me the superb collection of paintings in the picture gallery when my attention was taken by a portrait of a striking woman. What was curious about this picture was that the canvas was punctured by hundreds of tiny holes, almost as though woodworm had been busy.

'That's a Goya. It's rather fine, isn't it?' the Duchess remarked when she saw my interest.

'It is magnificent,' I agreed. 'But what are all those holes?'

'Oh, that's the children's fault. For some reason they never liked that picture, and so they used to throw darts at it.'

During the making of *Lawrence of Arabia* I worked in a number of fine buildings in Spain. We used the splendid Moorish Alcazar, and also an enormous quasi-Egyptian building which had been put up for a great exhibition due to be held in 1936. The Spanish Civil War had intervened and so the exhibition was never held. The building, however, proved an ideal substitute for Allenby's headquarters in Cairo, with its sweeping colonnades and vast areas of marble floor.

David Lean, the director—we had worked together making *The Bridge on the River Kwai*—was particularly enchanted by the effect of military boots clattering on this marble. He insisted that I had steel tips fitted to the heels and toes of my riding boots, and I always had to wear my spurs rather loose. Every time I took a step, it sounded like knights in armour on the rampage.

During the film I became great friends with Peter O'Toole. We had never acted together before, but we got along extremely well. This seemed to concern David, and one day he took me aside.

'Jack,' he said bluntly. 'I'm worried.'

'What's the trouble?' I asked him.

'Allenby,' he replied, 'is a father figure.'

I agreed. 'So?'

'So, you must be aloof, and you appear to be very friendly with Peter.'

I said, yes, indeed I was—we had a lot in common. 'We are both experienced actors, and what we do socially is not going to interfere with our acting.'

'Even so, I think you should be careful that your friendship does not intrude into your performance,' he said. For a brilliant film director, I thought that this was an extraordinary observation, and I ignored his advice, because I couldn't see the point of it. The fact that we used to have some rousing sessions together in no way impinged on our work; maybe it even improved our performances.

Unfortunately, my performance as Allenby attracted a good deal of criticism from the Allenby family. After the première, Lady Allenby of Wittersham was quoted as saying: 'Mr Hawkins' portrayal of my father-in-law shows a monster—not a great man. ... It is most distressing for the family, who loved and respected him, to know that his character is being distorted in this way.'

At the time, I answered the charges with the comment: 'I agree that the character has been slanted slightly, but Lady Allenby must remember that this is a film about Lawrence—not the Field-Marshal.'

The criticism was based on the way that the film treated the famous Foreign Office document which set out how the Middle East was to be partitioned following the destruction of the old Turkish Empire. In fact, Allenby knew nothing about the secret document, but the film implied duplicity in his dealings with the Arabs.

I feel personally that the Allenby family did have grounds for complaint, and since I had read every book I could find on the man before I played the role, I was less than happy with the film's account of events. I had some fairly heavy arguments about this slanting of truth, but inevitably, if you start introducing little-known facts about the character you are playing, somebody is going to say: 'That's all very fine, but filmically it will be better done our way.'

This is usually undeniable, and so the argument comes down to two choices. Either you say: 'Give the part to somebody else, I'm going home,' which is difficult, and usually expensive—if not impossible—since you have signed a contract to play the role and play it in the way they want it; or else you knuckle down, swallow your annoyance, and get on with the job.

As it happened, I was able to get my own way quite a lot as we went along during the actual shooting, but the skill of the cutting rooms was used to turn scenes back into the pattern originally conceived. After the first week of the film being shown in London there were complaints that it was too long, and one of my favourite scenes was cut out completely, although shots of sky and sand remained, which were lovely to see, but then this is one of the hazards of filming.

Another, more uncomfortable hazard was that for six months I went around with a shaven head. I remember going to meet Dee—who had no idea of this—when she landed at Seville Airport. I had been forced to buy a flat cap, simply to keep my head warm, and her look of horror when I removed this in the hotel lift going up to our room made me realise how terrible I must look. The reason for removing all my hair was that Allenby had been a baldish man. So I was shaved and given a hair-piece of wispy dark hair, which was stuck on to my bald pate daily. Stanley Hall, of Wig Creations, also made me a second clever hair-piece, the same as my own hair.

Sometimes when Dee and I went out to dinner, she used to stick this on for me (with Johnson's Adhesive). There were thus a lot of more than usually confused waiters in Seville, for sometimes I appeared totally bald and yet the next night would arrive with a thick black thatch of curly hair—and no explanation.

Peter and I worked together again afterwards in *Lord Jim*. I played Captain Marlowe, which is quite a short part, but I also narrated the film. When I was first offered the part I asked to see the script, but was told there were only a few copies, and the director was not willing to let these out of his hands. Naturally, I insisted on seeing one, and after some discussion it was agreed that a copy would be sent to my home at Roehampton. That same afternoon a chauffeur arrived in a limousine, and delivered the script to my front door. I thanked him and said I would return it some time the next day.

'No, sir,' he said. 'I have instructions to wait until you have finished with it.'

So he waited patiently while I read the script, put it back in its envelope, and handed it over to him.

In fact the script differed very little from the book by Joseph Conrad, which I could have bought from the local newsagent for a few shillings in paperback. Finally, I agreed to make the film, particularly as it was being shot in Hong Kong, and I thought that the location would make a nice trip for Dee. As events turned out, this proved a very agreeable holiday for both of us.

For the first ten days after we arrived, I did not do a stroke of work, but every morning I used to go into the production office that Columbia had set up and ask if there was a copy of the script that I could have.

The girls in the office would giggle and say: 'Afraid not, Mr Hawkins. Perhaps tomorrow.' The thing was being guarded like the Gothenburg Bible.

Noel Purcell, that wonderfully talented Irish actor, who a few years previously had carted me round the Curragh in Ireland at a race-meeting, filling me up with drinks and marking my card with eight consecutive losers, arrived to play a small part. Wisely, he had occupied himself on the long journey from Dublin by sampling the hospitality of the airline, so that when he was met by the Press at Hong Kong and asked how long he was staying, he simply pulled a tatty scrap of paper from his pocket, and said: 'All I can tell you is that I have flown thousands of bloody miles to do this.' Ten lines of dialogue were typed on the paper, but at least he had a script or, to be accurate, the part of the script that concerned him, while I had nothing.

Noel is, of course, an Irishman, but he is also something of a professional Irishman, with all the charm of his kind. Another professional Irishman who, before I met him, I was told ate Englishmen for breakfast, is John Ford, the great director, who is perhaps best known for his classic Western, *Stagecoach*.

I made *Gideon's Day*, a Scotland Yard thriller, with him and grew devoted to him because he was a perfect actor's director. He loathed front-office types, and if any accountant or such non-artistic hireling had the temerity to set foot on the set while we were working, John would call everything to a halt and walk off until the man left. He refused to work if any of the management were present. This was a cunning ploy, because when a film is halted the delay costs a great deal of money, and this fact acted as a most successful deterrent to uninvited visitors.

At first meeting, Ford's appearance could be a trifle alarming. He wore a black patch over one eye and a greasy, battered trilby. I was told that the patch and the hat had been with him for at least fifty years. There were also odd little bursts of inexplicable eccentricity that one had to accept. I think it was on the first day of shooting that he picked on a scene, consisting of about four pages of dialogue, and said: 'What are all these God-damned lines about? We'll say them all together.' We then had to chant them in unison. I still don't know whether this was some strange joke, or a peculiar psychological idea that he thought helpful, but it didn't seem to achieve anything either way.

129

Although, in the past, Ford had the reputation of being a fairly heavy drinker, at the time of making this film he was on the wagon, and fairly virulent about people who did drink. I had been warned to be cautious, but I was not going to change the habits of a lifetime just to suit the whim of one director.

After the community reading, Ford turned to me.

'I shan't want you until this afternoon,' he announced. 'Go and have some lunch.'

I said: 'Thank you,' and was just about to leave the set when he asked: 'Where are you going?'

There was a silence when I replied: 'To a pub across the road.'

'Are you going to drink?'

'Yes.'

'What are you going to have?'

'A gin and tonic, I should think.'

'In that case,' he said, 'have one for me.'

When I got back, John was sitting in his director's chair.

'How was lunch?' he asked.

'Fine,' I said. 'Fine.'

'And how was the drink?'

'Very nice.'

'You put too much tonic in mine.'

This patter became a kind of daily running gag. Sometimes he would slightly vary it by saying: 'I think I feel like a couple, today.' I liked working with him, and he knew his business backwards. When John Ford said a take was good, you knew it was.

There was one rather tricky little scene, I remember, that took quite a time to get right, but eventually it was shot and sent off to be processed. He was pleased with the result, and invited me to have some 'chomoke', which was the name he always used for coffee. While we were drinking it, Freddie Young, one of the really great cameramen—and now a considerable director in his own right—was prowling all over the set with his viewfinder.

Eventually, John asked him what he was doing. Freddie, who is a very intense and meticulous character, replied: 'I think we should do that scene from another angle.'

130

'For Chrissake, come off the set, we finished that scene half an hour ago.' And nothing would make John Ford change his mind.

I think one thing delighted him above all others in making *Gideon's Day*; a guided tour of Scotland Yard was arranged for us. Here the thing that really caught his fancy was that every spare level surface seemed to have a cup of tea parked on it. He mentioned this to the senior police officer who was showing us around, and later he was asked if tea-cups could be kept out of the film. Obviously, it was thought that they did not give a very good impression of what is possibly the best-known police headquarters in the world.

Solemnly, John said that he quite understood, but his Irish sense of mischief got the better of him, for when the film appeared, every desk, shelf and filing-cabinet in Scotland Yard carried its ubiquitous cup and saucer!

There are few films that I cannot look back on without finding some reason for pleasure, or pride, or at least, amusement, but there is one strong exception—*Zulu*. Financially, it was a great success, and nobody can deny that it was good entertainment, but as an actor I felt let down. Indeed, in many respects I believe I was cheated out of a good performance.

The film told the story of Rorke's Drift in Africa, where a hundred British soldiers fought off 3,000 Zulu warriors. I was offered the part of a Swiss Lutheran missionary, Otto Wit, which was an unusual one for me to play in a war film, for Wit was a pacifist who attempted to prevent the wholesale slaughter of the warriors. Largely because it was so unlike all the parts I was well known for, it appealed to me, and before we went to South Africa on location I discussed the role, and the way I thought it should be played, in great detail with the producer, Cy Enfeld.

What I did not know then was that Cy is a great prestidigitator, a man who, in the kindest interpretation of the word, is a skilled conjurer. Had I realised this I might have been rather more careful but, as it was, I believed that my interpretation of the role was being taken seriously, and so I played it with this conviction.

During my scenes, Cy had arranged a number of covering shots which, for example, showed various other characters laughing at me; in other words, sending me up as a misguided buffoon. The performance that appeared on the screen bore no relationship whatever to the performance I gave in front of the cameras. When I saw it on the first night, I was so annoyed that I got out of my seat and walked out of the cinema—the only time I have ever walked out on any première.

However, thinking of my friends, Stanley Baker and Michael Caine—and of my astonished wife, left alone in the front row of the circle—I recovered my good humour sufficiently to collect her and take her on to the traditional first-night party. All my protests achieved was that Dee thought I must have suddenly been taken ill, and everyone else—if they thought anything at all—believed I'd simply gone to the loo!

Fortunately, the sort of situation that prompted these feelings has been rare in my career. Indeed, if I have to pick a film I have made which was the complete opposite to the *Zulu* fiasco I would settle on *Man in the Sky* just for one scene.

This was a film in which I played a test pilot. In the first scene we shot I had to land an aircraft that had developed a serious fault in mid-air and then, in the most humdrum way, climb into my car, stop to pick up some laundry, make my way home—to a semi-detached on the edge of Wolverhampton—and start to run a bath.

My wife, beautifully played by Elizabeth Sellars, asks me how the day has gone, and I said 'all right' in an off-hand manner. Unknown to me she had witnessed the near-disaster, and she rounds on me, accusing me of being prepared to sacrifice her and our children simply for my job.

I then had a six-minute speech, which was really the justification why a man does a job—any job—which was brilliantly written by Bill Rose, one of the finest screen-writers, and a man who wrote perfectly for me.

This speech attracted a lot of attention, and for an actor no feeling exceeds the satisfaction when people come up afterwards and say that the character you played was splendid, and you were the right person to play it.

The only drawback was that I had to spend twelve weeks on location in Wolverhampton. It always amused me that, while my wife could manage to visit me in locations all over the globe, she curiously enough could only make one weekend in Wolverhampton!

Dee's excuse was that the children were all having measles in turn.

# ELEVEN

For thirteen years after finishing *Bonnie Prince Charlie*, I made films almost continuously, although there were occasional breaks when I returned to the theatre, such as the unfortunate *Romeo and Juliet* in New York, and the much more successful duet of Christopher Fry plays in London, *A Phoenix too Frequent*, and *Thor, With Angels*—at the Lyric, in which I played Thor.

When I first became seriously involved in films at the end of the war the industry was booming. Many people went to their local cinema two or three times every week; and even small towns had at least two cinemas so the demand for films was very high. Audiences queued patiently for seats and financial investment in films was regarded as almost blue chip.

Unfortunately, even at that prosperous time, the gathering warning signs were largely ignored, although a few men like Alex Korda had the foresight in the early 1950s to realise that decent films could and must be made on reasonable budgets, if for no other reason than to make better use of the vast and expensive resources of the studios.

He had the clever idea of converting successful West End plays into films—virtually as they stood—without expensive locations, which could be shot in about ten days, a time that was then considered almost impossibly short. I made one with Margaret Leighton and Ralph Richardson—*Home at Seven* by J. B. Priestley. Unfortunately, we ran out of plays, so the system was not pursued to the logical conclusion of the low-budget films that are being made today.

At that time, I was still under contract to Korda, but made very few films for him because he preferred to hire me out, at a profit, to other companies, so I worked almost constantly at Ealing

Studios and Pinewood—*Home at Seven*, being an exception, was filmed at Shepperton, Alex's studios.

After *Mandy* and during the filming of *The Cruel Sea*, I had a surprise approach over Sunday lunch from a friend in the Rank Organisation who offered me a long contract at a princely salary, simply on the rushes they had seen of *The Cruel Sea*. While I was loath to leave Alex, being genuinely fond of him, as well as respecting his talent, Dee and I decided that the security of the Rank offer was very important to us in view of our growing family—but how to break this news to Korda?

The deed was done by our friend Bill O'Bryen, but Korda, never one to admit defeat easily, insisted that I should see him. I literally had no time because I was filming, but Alex was adamant, and finally we met for breakfast at Claridges where he lived in great style.

I had no heart for this interview, or stomach for the meal, and Dee's parting words as I left home were: 'Don't let him change your mind—we know the fatal charm the man has!'

Our confrontation proved to be more battle than breakfast, for Korda was at his most persuasive: it was unwise for actors to be tied to contracts—although he had bound me pretty tightly himself; I could choose my own scripts, my own leading ladies, even my own price, and so on.

But I remained firm, pointing out that in the years I had been contracted to him, he had made very little use of me and, in fact, this was only the second time I had been invited to meet him socially.

Korda's final salvo was: 'But, dear Jack, you can't go and work for that bloody miller.'

I pointed out that I wasn't going to work in the flour mills of Joseph Rank, but at his brother, J. Arthur's, studios.

Sadly, Alex shook his head.

'Dear Jack,' he said. 'Good luck. I am the man who had a golden sovereign in his pocket and did not know it.'

There is an ironic epilogue to all this. As soon as I had signed with Rank, they hired me out in exactly the same way, but this time to American companies!

By 1959, when I was receiving a fee of around £30,000 a film, the growing impact of television, which provided visual entertainment without the need to leave your living-room, plunged the film industry into financial chaos. Like many other leading actors and actresses, I agreed to take a cut in salary. In my case the cut was about £10,000 a film, and in exchange I received a share in any profits the picture made.

Naturally, these profits cannot be guaranteed, and the move made some of us apprehensive for the future, but in retrospect it was a valuable catalyst. It aroused my interest in production and, more than anything else, it forced me to recognise television as genuine competition, and not some kind of fairground sideshow, which I think was how many of we more established actors and actresses regarded it. I fear we had a rather arrogant attitude to the small screen, thinking, somewhat foolishly, that it was a little beneath our dignity to perform on it.

My first appearance on the box was in a play by Fritz Hochwaelder, called *The Public Prosecutor*, about the reign of terror during the French Revolution. I was so impressed by it that I bought the stage rights. Television, I was beginning to realise, is rather like breathing. You can't ignore it. Also, it is a superlative advertising medium, and brings one's name and face into almost every home in the country.

I repeated my performance as King Magnus in *The Applecart* at Dee's suggestion, who felt it had not been seen by enough people at the Arts Theatre Club. Now, millions saw it—and it was very highly praised. I became involved with a TV series, *The Four Just Men* based, I believe, on the Edgar Wallace stories, and this turned out quite well, largely because we had first-class British feature film writers. William Fairchild and Janet Green—with Basil Dearden directing. And fine actors—Richard Conte, Dan Dailey and Vittorio de Sica—playing the other three Just Men.

We were a kind of four-man commando committed to undertake the defence of any human being in trouble—and this meant a certain sameness in the plots. I was therefore relieved when Carl

Foreman sent me the script of a film to be called *League of Gentlemen*.

No actor could have been other than excited by this brilliantly written story of an ex-army officer who collects a group of his former war-time comrades to plan and carry out a daring bank robbery. Certainly, this made a welcome change from the crusading atmosphere of *The Four Just Men*.

I would add in passing that this TV series provided another chance for me to show my ill-luck in financial affairs. Remembering Bill Holden's *coup* in *Kwai*, I decided to take a lower fee but a share of the profits. Alas, there were none. The company went broke!

I told Carl Foreman right away how excited I was about his script.

'This is tremendous,' I said. 'I want to do it.'

But Carl was in the middle of another film, and said he did not think he could set up a production for some time. Meanwhile, I had shown the script to Basil Dearden, who I was working with daily, and he took it home with him. The following morning, when I arrived at the studios, the first thing he did was to hand me back the script and say: 'Jack, you have got to let me do this.'

'That's all very well,' I replied. 'But I haven't been offered a part myself yet, and it looks as though there may be some difficulty and delay in setting up the production.'

Later, we sat down and thrashed out the problems, with the result that we decided to set up our own production company. Bryan Forbes had written the script and he and Richard Attenborough were in partnership, so they came in. We were also joined by Michael Relph, who was an associate of Basil's. We put a few thousand pounds each into the kitty and launched ourselves as Allied Film Makers.

We worked out a distribution guarantee with Rank, and obtained a large loan from the National Provincial Bank, and by the time we had finished these negotiations our modest initial sum had grown to £1,000,000. We then bought the rights of the film from Carl Foreman, who prudently retained a little of the action himself.

It was a tremendously entertaining film to make, in spite of the fact that my throat began to cause me some trouble because we had a long sequence in a smoke-screen, and this took two days to shoot. But my hoarseness was nothing—or so it seemed then—compared with the excitement of having real control over the whole film.

For once, one was responsible for a complete film, and not just playing a part to the best of one's ability. And, of course, the satisfaction of creating a complete thing was spiced with the gamble involved, because trying to make a fortune out of a film is not so very far removed from trying to win a football pool. The chances of success are about the same. But, as things turned out, the film was a tremendous box-office success.

Looking back, I realise now I had been over-working for too long. One of the problems of being a successful actor is that you are either 'hot' or 'cold', and at that time I was extremely 'hot'. Offers poured in from all sides and one could never resist the temptation to accept challenging parts.

One of them came after I had finished *The Four Just Men*: the part of the butler in *Fallen Idol* which Ralph Richardson had played in Carol Reed's film when I played a small part just after the war. I decided to accept, and this meant going to New York, which Dee and I always enjoy. It wasn't until I arrived that I discovered that the actress playing opposite me was my former wife, Jessica Tandy.

Fortunately, we all three found the situation rather amusing. I had not seen her for nine years but had been sent a cutting of a newspaper interview in which she said, when asked a question about me and our marriage: 'Jack Hawkins is a wonderful actor, but a rotten husband.' I am glad she didn't put the adjectives the other way round!

Dee and I came home by sea, simply to give me a much-needed break before starting *League of Gentlemen*, leaving behind a lot of tempting offers from Hollywood.

Now that I am unable to do television work on any great scale, I sometimes wish I had taken the medium more seriously when I had the chance, but unfortunately, or perhaps fortunately, one cannot foresee the future. Even so, I was lucky in the plays I did, like Shaw's *Caesar and Cleopatra* for NBC. It would also obviously have been profitable for me because as long ago as 1963 I was paid £10,000 for a sixty-minute TV play *To Bury Caesar*, which was jointly produced by the BBC and NBC.

That was also the year in which I joined forces with Dame Peggy Ashcroft, Anthony Asquith, Sir John Betjeman, Dame Edith Evans, Ivan Foxwell, Miss Rose Heilbron, QC, Sir Bernard Miles, Jacquetta Hawkes (Mrs J. B. Priestley), Sir Michael Redgrave, Dame Flora Robson, Sir John Rothenstein and Peter Ustinov in a bid for a contract to run an independent television company. We were unsuccessful, but I suspect we would have made a formidable impact on television drama, had we been given the franchise.

Apart from the bleak episodes I made for *Dr Kildare*, the last important television play in which I acted was *The Trial and Torture of Sir John Rampayne*. For me, this was a personal trial and torture, for it was then I realised I had more than a sore throat; I had cancer.

# TWELVE

Since I was sixteen or seventeen, I have always been troubled with a slight weakness of my throat. I remember when I was in New York in *Journey's End* I suffered the first serious bout of trouble with it. I woke up one morning feeling as though half a pineapple was wedged against my Adam's Apple, and with no idea why this should be.

For a couple of days I managed to struggle through the performances, and then the management called in a doctor. He took one look down my throat.

'What the hell have you been doing?' he asked.

I croaked something about 'the usual things'.

'In that case,' he said. 'Don't start on the unusual.'

He gave me something to ease the discomfort, and after a few days' rest I was back to normal.

Being young, I did not give much thought to the trouble, although over the years, whenever I caught a cold or any kind of infection, it seemed to go straight to my throat. But I put this down to the fact that as an actor I used my voice more strenuously than most people, except perhaps school teachers.

It was not until I was making *League of Gentlemen* that, as I have explained, my throat began to give more serious trouble. At first this manifested itself in a feeling of discomfort and a general voice weakness. I expected it to pass off, suspecting it was probably laryngitis, and gargled and sucked soothing lozenges, but the pain did not leave me, and nothing could relieve it. Instead, it grew progressively worse.

Finally, I went to see my doctor, who recommended me to a throat specialist. He suggested I should go into hospital and have a full clinical examination conducted under a general anaesthetic so that the larynx could be scraped and laboratory tests made to discover exactly what was causing the trouble.

A short while after the examination I was told that there was what the doctors delicately called 'a condition' present, but that this could be put right by cobalt treatment. The doctors seemed so sure that they could cure me with this treatment that they gave me great confidence, and I decided to go ahead.

For the next few weeks, I received the treatment. This had to be a very closely guarded secret, because if word leaked out that I was suffering from a serious throat complaint, possibly even cancer, it was very unlikely that any film company or theatre management would hire me. Actors are generally insured before they take on starring roles, and obviously no insurance company would consider me a safe risk.

Dee and I had another reason for secrecy: our two sons were at boarding school, and we did not want to risk alarming them should they read something about this in a newspaper.

So, three times every week, I used to slip into the Royal Marsden Hospital through the back entrance, and make my way to the treatment room. This looked like something out of a science fiction film. I would be strapped to a padded bench, while a great instrument with a robot eye hovered above me. My head was held rigid in a special clamp, and the point of my throat to be treated was marked out with a kind of indelible pencil. The machine's 'eye' would be positioned just over the spot, and then the staff would retreat behind a lead and glass screen.

For a few moments there would be silence, and then a clonking sound that came closer and closer—presumably the cobalt moving up the tube towards the 'eye'. When there was a click I knew it had arrived, and for the next five minutes the invisible rays would do their damnedest to destroy the growth. Then there would be another click and I would hear the cobalt retreating back down the pipe, its work done for that day.

There was no pain involved, but the treatment did have the most depressing effect on my outlook; I felt encompassed by gloom in a way and to an extent I had never before experienced.

141

Once the course of treatment had been completed, Dee and I escaped to Italy.

This was an almost unbearably anxious time, only made tolerable by Dee's patience and encouragement, and the tranquillity and sunshine of Italy. I even rediscovered the pleasure of painting, a hobby I had toyed with as a young man, but abandoned years before, when filming took up most of my time.

A bitter disappointment was that, because of my throat, I had to abandon a return to the stage in a play, *The Lizard on the Rock*. Altogether, I took nearly eight months to recover from the treatment, but in the end my voice returned to normal. To make quite certain that I was not straining it more than I had to, I took voice production lessons, and cut the number of cigarettes I smoked each day from about sixty to five.

When my voice had returned to its usual strength, and there was no pain or discomfort in my throat, I felt elated. I had, so I believed, beaten cancer, and armed with this confident belief I supposed I worked too hard, partly in relief at my incredible escape, and partly because, subconsciously, I wondered whether good health would—could—last.

I felt fit in every way, and when I had a slight sore throat about five years after the cobalt treatment, I went to my throat specialist, and he gave me a thorough examination.

'It does look a bit rough,' he admitted. 'How long is it since you had the treatment?'

'About five years,' I replied.

'In that case, you've got nothing to worry about. But just give your throat a bit of a rest. Otherwise, you are in the clear, no trouble at all.'

Perhaps, as I say, in the back of my mind there still lingered the nagging doubt that the cobalt treatment had not been completely successful, because even after this visit to the specialist I worked to the limit, going from one major film to another with barely a week's rest in between.

One thing I knew for certain was that if there were a repetition of the trouble then I could not be treated again with cobalt radiation. This is one of those experiences for which the body has only a certain degree of tolerance. If I had a recurrence, surgery would be the only course left. And major surgery to an actor's throat meant the loss of his voice; and with the actor's voice goes the actor's livelihood.

Apart from this one relapse, all went well until 1964, when I was making *The Guns of Batasi* with Richard Attenborough and Dame Flora Robson. I was playing one of my familiar old Army characters again, and suddenly my throat started to play up; it felt raw and rough, and gradually I began to lose my voice.

This time I really could not bear to face the doctors. There was no question of more cobalt treatment, and I suppose I was quite simply frightened of being given more deadly diagnosis. A number of friends had told me about a faith healer who, they said, had achieved some seemingly miraculous cures. Frankly, I have never been much inclined towards faith healers, but I felt desperate, and as a a last resort decided to consult him.

He was very encouraging, and assured me that all would be fine. I went through the laying-on of hands, the praying and meditation, and certainly all this seemed to have some soothing psychological effect, because for a few months following these visits I felt fit and well, and my cheerfulness returned. But then organically the cancer took over.

I managed a couple more films—*Judith*, with Sophia Loren and Peter Finch, and *Masquerade*, which was directed by my old friend Basil Dearden—and even a charity appearance in a UN film about drug trafficking, called *The Poppy is also a Flower*. My voice was more or less on the edge during the shooting of this last film, for which I was paid £1, but somehow I managed to get through it.

I came back from the South of France, where we had made the film, to rehearse for the television play I have already mentioned, *The Trial and Torture of Sir John Rampayne*. This was a fearful trial and torture for me. Every rehearsal at the dreary drill hall in Wandsworth which we had hired became an act of endurance. About two days before we were due to put on the play live we were rehearsing a crowd scene, when I was suddenly seized with a coughing fit. To my alarm, I felt my mouth fill with warm liquid. I took a tissue out of my pocket and wiped my lips. The tissue was red with blood.

Somehow, God knows how, I managed to finish the scene before rushing off to the loo to clear my throat. This time I was seriously alarmed. I finished the day's rehearsing, climbed into my car and drove straight home to Roehampton. I must have looked as dreadful as I felt, because when I was at the drinks cupboard, pouring myself a large brandy, Dee came into the room and asked: 'What's the matter with you?'

'I think we had better call the doctor,' I said, and told her what had happened. Later that evening, our family doctor arrived with a throat specialist. They both had a thoroughly good look down my throat and conferred for some time before delivering a verdict.

'One thing we are certain of, and that is the trouble is not cancer,' they assured me. 'Cancer doesn't behave like this. We can only think that you have somehow ruptured a blood vessel in your throat.'

So, once again, hope.

Someone stood in for me at the dress rehearsal of the TV play, but I was able to go through with the actual public performance, with the aid of pain-killing injections given to me by my throat specialist.

It was while I was having a few days' rest in bed afterwards that I received the offer to do the *Dr Kildare* episodes. Reassured by what the doctors had told me, I made my fateful trip to Hollywood for what was my last truly speaking part.

When I returned to London I was in considerable pain, my voice was a travesty of what it had been, so I lost no time in visiting my throat specialist again. He sent me to University Hospital in London, to see a brilliant Australian surgeon, Myles Formby.

Once again, I was given a direct examination under an anaesthetic, and the specimens taken from my larynx were passed on to the hospital laboratory. I had to wait two days for the results: two days in a small hospital room waiting for a verdict which, if it was what I feared it would be, carried no hope of any appeal.

As I have already described, the verdict was cancer. I could either struggle on as I was and die, or I could have the operation that would kill my career but give me a further lease of life. There was only one decision, and although I knew little of the real implications of the operation, I think that the one consideration uppermost in my mind during the following days was that the operation in all probability would end the terrible pain in my throat.

I suppose I was rather like a man whose leg has been horribly crushed in a motor accident. When the surgeon tells him that he is going to operate and put an end to the agony, the victim thinks only of this, and not of the fact that he is going to lose his leg for ever.

All I wanted to do, once I had made up my mind to go ahead with the laryngectomy, was to get it over and done with. My poor secretary was therefore under instructions to pester the hospital for a firm date for my readmission.

When she made her first call to Myles' office on the day following the verdict she was told: 'Mr Hawkins must be patient. He must realise that a theatre has to be booked, anaesthetist engaged and theatre sisters made available.'

'MR HAWKINS MUST BE PATIENT.'

This was an impossible request, because Mr Hawkins was afraid of waiting, afraid of having more time to think, afraid of being tempted to retract.

At last, the word came! I was to report to the hospital on the next Friday evening to be ready for the operation, scheduled for the Saturday afternoon. Dee drove me to the hospital, and we shared half a bottle of champagne in my room before she left, smiling and cheerful, never for one moment revealing the unhappiness she was feeling for me, and of course, for both of us. We had not said much, for there was really nothing left to say. This operation would mark the end of one career; would it also signal the beginning of another?

For five hours, the surgeons worked on my throat, cutting away the cancerous tissue and building a new system through which in future I would breathe and speak. But it was many hours before I returned to consciousness, and when finally my mind cleared a little, I found myself looking up through a tracery of tubes and pipes all leading one way—into me. I felt like a rather absurd but sophisticated piece of plumbing. Bandages were wrapped tightly round my throat, but I felt no pain from the operation wound. The only discomfort came from a piece of metal in my nose.

'What the hell has happened to me?' I thought, but when I opened my mouth to ask myself the question out loud, I could only make a ghastly, gurgling, hissing sound that emerged from the tube in my throat. The answer was, at that moment, all too clear: Jack Hawkins, as an actor, was dead.

Under normal circumstances, I am sure that such a thought would have overwhelmed me, but fortunately nature is surprisingly merciful to the sick, and cunningly deflects their minds from utter desperation. During the two days that followed the operation I seemed to live in a trance-like state, half-way between sleep and wakefulness, in which dreams and images diverted my thoughts.

It is curious that in moments of great stress, such as the postoperative stage, one becomes obsessed by strange desires. Mine was to have a grilled Dover sole for breakfast on that first morning after the operation. I had two private nurses, both Australians—Nurse Jones by day and Nurse Cameron at night—and when I wrote out my request for grilled Dover sole on a pad by my bedside, Nurse Jones read it, smiled gently and then mixed a jugful of Complan and poured it down the tube in my nose.

Although I think they must sometimes have looked on me as a rather tiresome old geriatric, both those nurses were superb. Somehow they managed to make me feel that I had undergone little worse than an operation to remove my appendix. I was never permitted to feel sorry for myself, and I realise now how greatly this helped me to recover and face the problems that confronted me.

They never disapproved of the little stock of champagne that I kept in my room, although I suspect I was breaking some kind of hospital rule, but at the same time they made no special exceptions for me, just because I was a film star. I was still expected to be an obedient patient, although I was constantly surprised at the orders that were sometimes given to me.

On the day after the operation I was told sharply to get out of bed and sit in the visitors' chair.

'You must be mad,' I thought, and indeed I would have said so had I been able to speak. But I obeyed orders, my bed was made and in a rather zombie-like manner I thankfully climbed back into it again. I felt quite pleased that I had achieved this independent movement, so that when the call of nature became pressing I started to get out of bed again, only to be stopped by a stentorian voice demanding: 'What do you think you are doing, Mr Hawkins?'

I managed to convey that I wanted to go to the loo, and that the need was urgent.

'Oh, no you don't. Get back into bed,' the nurse said, and shot out of the room to fetch a bedpan. But had she moved with the speed of Batman it would not have been fast enough, such was my extremity, so by the time she returned I was enthroned.

'No, Mr Hawkins, no!' she exclaimed indignantly when she returned.

I have yet to discover why spurning the bedpan is held to be some kind of subtle insult to the nursing profession. In fact, I would not have consciously insulted any of the staff who looked after me during those post-operative days, with the possible exception of the physiotherapist!

She arrived in my room on the day after the operation and began to pummel me in the most ferocious way, and did not seem satisfied until I began to cough. I obviously could not say anything, but I scribbled down a long complaining note. I was told that the massage, as it was delicately described, was essential in order to keep my lungs clear. So, the physiotherapist was working for my well-being and not satisfying some odd sadistic urge.

Despite the assurance, I cannot say that I looked forward to her visits, but they were obviously important to my recovery.

Throughout these days, throughout the frustrations and irritations that I jotted down on my writing pad, throughout the worry and the uncertainty about the future, Dee never appeared other than unruffled and happy when she was with me.

Even after the operation, and the hours of waiting for news from the surgeon, she was able to face the Press and make this buoyant statement: 'He came through the long operation remarkably well. When I saw him afterwards, he was out of bed walking around. Now, it is mainly discomfort. Already, he is taking physiotherapy for breathing, and finds this a bit exhausting. Of course, he will have to learn to speak again, but that should not be difficult for an actor trained in breath control. After he comes out of hospital we shall have to continue the therapy. We shall go to France. After that, we shall discuss the future. He may be doing some production. I should say he will be out of action for about three months. The important thing is that the malignant growth was in a place which was operable, and I am pleased to say it was successful.'

# THIRTEEN

It was the feeling that in some way I had lost complete control of my bodily functions, at least in part, that depressed me most of all during these first few days after the operation.

I found, for example, that my nose ran continually, and I could do nothing about it other than keep mopping it. To blow it was out of the question: I could not even take a good sniff. Suddenly, this small irritation, the inability to do something that everyone else takes for granted, made me realise the full enormity of what had happened to me. I had, until then, taken good health and a strong physique for granted. Now, I could take nothing for granted any more.

I do not know what it was that eventually pulled me together. Maybe it was simply the knowledge that I was still alive; that I was not going to die of cancer, and that, anyway, things must get better, because nothing could be worse than the condition I was in.

Of course, there were other things. Dee I have already written about, but my friends also rallied around me. David Niven, in particular, was a tower of strength. He seemed determined to keep me cheerful at all costs, and was a constant and always welcome visitor. He had suffered great personal tragedy with the loss of his first wife, and I am certain he understood the anguish I was undergoing.

He has an infectious gaiety, and an extremely colourful sense of humour, both of which buoyed me up immensely. I remember him popping in one day and saying: 'You must hear this. I've just copied down this graffiti from a lavatory wall.'

He read from a scrap of paper: 'My mother made me a

homosexual.' Then he added: 'Someone else has written underneath, "If I get the wool, will she make me one, too?" '

I replied on my pad with my own graffiti story. One Christmas, on visiting the gents of a pub Dee and I used to go to, which was famous for the artistic obscenities, messages and sexual artwork on the walls, one joker had written in huge letters: 'Happy Christmas to all my readers.'

Flowers arrived in such quantities that before long it was difficult to decide whether my room looked like a dressing-room or a funeral parlour. I also received an enormous number of letters, many from old friends, and also a lot from strangers who had been through the same operation. They told me not to worry, because I would be all right, and I WOULD be able to speak again. These were a tremendous help and comfort, because although people in the hospital assured me all would be well, there were moments when I thought: 'It's no good. This is simply not going to work.'

But one person made quite sure that it was going to work, and that was the speech therapist who was sent to me. She was five feet of sheer determination. Failure was quite simply a word that did not feature in her vocabulary or even in her thoughts. She was the most tremendous bully, but a wonderful person. When we started our sessions she would thump me on the back and say: 'Relax, damn it. When you're taut, you can't talk at all.'

The technique I had to learn was to speak with my oesophagus, which is the tube through which one takes in food and drink. To do this I had to gulp down air, compress it to produce what is virtually a burp, and form that burp into a word. I cheated a bit, in an agreeable way, by using champagne to produce the burps.

I shall never forget the day when the speech therapist was just leaving the room, after a rather frustrating session, and I took a great gulp of champagne, and managed to come out with: 'This is damn good cham . . . pagne.'

Immediately she came running back into the room.

'God!' she said delightedly. 'He's *talking*.'

When I left hospital seventeen days after the operation I could speak ten consecutive words. Doreen and I fled from the bleak grey drabness of London in January to our little house at Cap Ferrat. There, in spring-like weather, and the peace that reigns during the off-season on the Riviera, I began the hard slog of learning to speak again.

The sounds that came grunting and hissing out of my throat were frightening to start with, particularly since every spluttering burst seemed only to serve as confirmation to me that I would never act again. But even in a situation like this there were compensations. As I became more and more proficient, and slowly and painfully increased my vocabulary, I experienced the indescribable thrill of being able to communicate by speech again. Not, it is true, in the melodious rounded tones of a practised verse speaker, but well enough for anyone to be able to understand me.

This was a long, hard struggle, but one that was probably easier for me to win than most people, because from a very early age I had been trained to use my voice to its fullest capacity. I can honestly say that I loved the sound of my own voice and, like all actors, I had never treated it in the way of other people, as just something that was there. I had learned to tune it, and to play it like an instrument.

Now that I had to start all over again, I was able to put those lessons learned so long ago to good use. Of course, I realised that I would never have a theatrical voice again, but I think I grew more articulate than many people might have been in the same situation.

During that difficult and often depressing time, I found that my thoughts frequently drifted back to when I had been making *Mandy*, and the weeks we spent on location in the school for deaf and dumb in Manchester. I remember the affection of those children, and the terrifying, incoherent sounds they made in their desperate eagerness to communicate. I knew now exactly how those little children must have felt; now I also experienced their frustrations and also the loneliness that comes with being unable to make yourself easily understood. But, above all, I remembered the devotion and superhuman patience of the teachers in that school in their agonisingly slow task of teaching the children to speak.

Just over a year after my operation, I was invited to open a new wing at the Hamilton Lodge School for Deaf Children in Brighton. I derived the most tremendous satisfaction from being told by some of the teachers afterwards that the children had told them they could understand my speech far better than those of the other speakers.

No doubt this was because I now have to use my lips much more clearly and definitely than before, and deaf people can read from my lips far more easily than from those of people with ordinary speech.

It took me nearly a year of solid hard work before I reached the point when I felt reasonably satisfied with the way I was speaking. When that goal was reached, I had to face up to my future, and frankly it did not look particularly bright or promising. I was an actor and acting was the only trade I knew, but now I had lost the instrument that was essential to the exercise of my craft. I felt like an old hulk that had been washed into some backwater without a rudder, masts or sails. Such were the gloomy thoughts that nagged at me as I planned and schemed at our home in Roehampton after our return from France.

Then, one day, entirely out of the blue, a visitor came to call, quite the least expected of our friends and acquaintances: Henry Hathaway, the director of *The Black Rose*, who had made everyone's life hell when we were filming it years before.

I had not seen him for a long time, but he came in and said: 'Jack, I want you and Doreen to come with me to Nairobi. I want you, Jack, to help me set up a film there.'

The film was *The Last Safari*, with Stewart Granger, and all I did was to act as a go-between for the company and the local actors. This was not a very taxing job, but it proved a tremendous boost to my confidence. Henry's was an act of compassion that demonstrated a sensitive understanding of other people's suffering. He had had cancer himself and he knew the anxiety and fear that it brings to the victim.

What I had also failed to appreciate was the determination of my friends and, above all, Dee, that I should not simply disappear from the scene. Indeed, but for Dee, pushing me along, I think I might have sat back and said, 'Well, that's that', but she refused to accept that I was finished, and so did many other good friends who rallied round with offers of work.

While I was in hospital I received a staggering number of letters from people asking if there was anything they could do to help, although at the time it did not seem as though anything could be done.

Henry was the first to take a hand in my future, and the next was Peter O'Toole, who came up with a part in *Great Catherine* by GBS, which he about to film. This contained the part of the British Ambassador to the Russian court, who is an idiotic, bumbling character, who never gets more than one or two words out before he is interrupted. Peter insisted that I play this part. So I was acting again and, in fact, using my new voice. I believe I am the only laryngectomy actor to do this and, of course, it was only possible in a part with so few words, most of them incomprehensible.

This was followed by an approach by Euan Lloyd, a producer with whom I had worked several times before. He insisted that I should play the part of an English nobleman in a western, *Shalako*, that he was making with Sean Connery and Brigitte Bardot. Perhaps these were not world-shattering parts in an histrionic sense, but the plain fact that I was given them at all had a marvellous effect on my morale. I knew now that I could build a new career as an actor without a voice.

I know that many ordinary people who have undergone the same operation have never been able to return to their old jobs, and have had a ghastly time rehabilitating themselves in other trades and professions, but theatre people are extraordinary. When you are fit and well and acting, they can be savagely critical and hurtful, but when something goes wrong, there is nothing they will not do to help you.

Those first steps, timidly taken, back into acting, have been followed by good roles in films like *Oh, What a Lovely War!*, in which I played the Emperor Franz Josef of Austria; *Nicholas and Alexandra*, which my old friend Sam Spiegel produced, where I was the Tsar's personal attendant; and the Headmaster of Harrow in *Young Winston*, through Carl Foreman and Richard Attenborough.

But there are times, inevitably I suppose, when I suffer great bouts of depression, usually when I fail to express what I really feel. For example, I can no longer laugh above a whisper, or give a good blast when I am angry! I also find I feel very frustrated when I see fellow actors of my generation going ahead with all sorts of exciting projects, acting in bigger and better plays, films and TV series, while I have to accept that these are impossible targets for me, because I am bounded on so many sides by restrictions.

It would be impossible for me to play in the live theatre again, and television is also difficult for, although many plays are recorded, they are recorded live, and not recorded and dubbed. Therefore, my field is fairly limited. In the films I make, my voice is dubbed, with great patience and brilliance, either by Charles Gray or by Robert Rietti.

What I have found interesting and rewarding has been the development of an entirely new technique of acting. In many ways, I have reverted to the days of the old silent films. Apart from rehearsals, where I do speak my lines to give the other actors some idea of timing, I am miming entirely, because I have found that for the actual shooting it is better for editing and dubbing if the technicians have an absolutely clear tape from me.

To compensate for what I have lost by having no theatrical voice, I act much more with my eyes. I know that many people find my voice worrying to listen to, simply because it sounds as though it is the most desperate agony to produce, but in fact it does not cause me any physical discomfort when I speak.

After I made a speech at the British film awards presentation, people came up to me and told me how brave I was, and they meant it. But there was nothing brave in trying to do my best.

154

I am quite blatant about this and apologise for the noise, but explain that it is the best they are going to get.

Of course, there are problems in ordinary social life which worried me initially. One difficulty is that I have to clear my throat from time to time, and this can become embarrassingly necessary at dinner and lunch parties. If I don't know my host or hostess very well, I explain that if I have to ask to be excused in the middle of the meal this has no reflection on the cooking, but simply that I must leave the room to clear my throat, which can be rather a noisy process.

Another difficulty is that one cannot eat and speak at the same time—not that one should anyway—but normally people can swallow quickly and then speak. Not me. I have to swallow slowly, and wait until the food is well and truly down before gulping air in order to speak.

A very dear friend of mine, John Rogerson, the racehorse owner, who had a laryngectomy some years before me, gave me a tip which I now always follow. Before going out to a dinner party, I eat a light snack at home so that I can ask for small portions at the table, and so have more time for talking.

I have also lost my sense of smell, and I can no longer swim, unless I plan to drown myself with the first plunge. Once a little girl, who saw me cavorting about in the Mediterranean with a rubber ring, asked my why I wore such a contraption.

'Because, if I don't, I would simply fill up with water and sink,' I told her.

She thought I was joking, but I wasn't.

But these are small losses compared with the gift of life that the skill of surgery has bestowed on me, and nothing compared with the love of my wife and family that I can still enjoy, and of course the wonderful knowledge that I can still work at the job that has given me so much happiness and pleasure.

I do not know what the future holds or whether, eventually, more surgery may be necessary. But if I were asked to choose a motto now it would come from Milton's *Comus*, a verse play in which I acted so many years ago in Regent's Park.

I pass on the words because they may well have meaning and comfort for others as well as for me.

> Yet where an equal poise of hope and fear
> Does arbitrate th' event, my nature is
> That I incline to hope, rather than fear.

# POSTSCRIPT

by Doreen Hawkins

Gatwick Airport, Easter Saturday, 1973. Cold and blustery, and I was on my way to New York without the feeling of anticipation and pleasure that I usually have when I am to make a journey, because I love travelling and I have a born wanderlust. I am happy in any craft that takes me anywhere.

But on the journey over I began to recognise this feeling of heaviness in my heart and a certain dread. I had experienced it once before during the flight to Los Angeles at the end of 1965, when I was on my way to join Jack whilst he was filming a sequence of *Dr Kildare*. He had telephoned me and I had packed and left at once, for I knew it was a cry for help. His voice was going and we both feared this might be for the last time.

It was a beautiful day when I arrived in New York and very hot. I was met by a representative of the Labarge Co. who manufactured the Voicbak, the device in which Jack had placed so much faith. Mr Bill Brantley, the Director of Communications, gave me a very warm greeting and was full of good news and optimism. He assured me I would find Jack in splendid spirits and health.

We made straight for the hospital, for I could hardly wait to see him and yet, when I entered the building, of which I was to see so much in later days, a feeling of foreboding clung to me.

When I got out of the lift on the seventh floor and started along the corridor, Jack was walking towards me looking very much himself apart from some strange new tube in his neck. It was marvellous to see him and we had many things to talk about, and momentarily my fears seemed to be quelled.

I met the doctors, Stanley Taub and Lloyd Bergner, who were enthusiastically planning the next stage of the operation. Both

157

were younger men than I expected—in their late thirties. We all had a drink. Jack was allowed to sip some Scotch, and an atmosphere of almost gaiety prevailed, but then I was told that Jack would not be able to leave with me that evening as we had previously arranged, but instead he could go on the following day. They gave me various instructions for liquid feeding and dressings. I was not at all prepared for this, for I am totally devoid of any nursing experience, apart from grazed knees and cuts with the children. Also, I felt depressed at the thought of going to Betty Bacall's apartment alone. Lauren Bacall is always known as Betty to her friends. She and I have been especially close, and she had generously loaned us her home.

I had known the apartment since she had first moved in after Humphrey Bogart's death. It is a lovely place overlooking Central Park, very big and spacious. Perhaps because I felt so tired by now —with the time change between New York and London it was quite late at night for me—an overwhelming sense of loneliness descended upon me, so I picked up a telephone in the hospital and rang to see if, by any chance, the maid was still there.

Instead, my call was answered by Steve, Betty's eldest son, who told me he was staying for the Easter weekend with his wife and baby and that Leslie, Betty's daughter, was also there. My spirits lifted at the thought of seeing them again, so I left Jack at the Flower and Fifth Avenue Hospital, and drove over to the apartment at Central Park West.

In later days, I never ceased to thank Betty and my luck for being in such a place. It is one of the oldest buildings in New York and very heavily guarded with a bevy of porters and electronically controlled gates to keep out all but the specially invited. During the next five weeks, I was to spend such a frighteningly lonely time that I was grateful for this protection.

When I rang the doorbell, Steve with the baby, and Leslie with a vast labrador, greeted me and made me immensely welcome. They were all getting ready to go off for an Easter celebration. I had not seen Steve since he was about twelve in England, because he was always away at school when I visited Betty in

New York, so we embraced fondly and happily. I was able to produce a present from his mother in the shape of a large woolly toy for his baby son. He called me Grandma from then on!

Leslie I have seen more frequently over the years. I think her so beautiful, her face shaped like her mother's, but with Bogie's colouring, her long dark hair streaming down her shoulders. We sat together and talked in the kitchen for a while. She is training to become a nurse and was therefore very interested in every aspect of Jack's operation, asking me many questions that I was simply unable to answer, knowing so little about it myself.

Finally, they all went. I was alone and suddenly realised how exhausted I was. I looked out over Central Park, at all the lights of New York twinkling, and remembered the marvellously exciting and happy times Jack and I had spent in the city, and how different my mood was now.

I could not rid myself of this strange premonition that somehow I was entering into the last act of some drama. I thought about Jack leaving home in such a hurry on that Sunday of 1st April—My God, April Fools' Day! Everything had all happened in such a rush. Although we had heard about this operation some two years before from Dustin Hoffmann, it was through an article in *The Sunday Times*, and the fact that Jack had some free time before filming again, that he had really thought seriously about investigating it further.

In his own impetuous way, in spite of feeble protests from me and one or two of our friends, he made the decision to fly to New York for discussions and return within four days. This seemed sensible and I agreed with it, because obviously he would not be satisfied until he had convinced himself one way or another whether it was worth while to take the risk, or indeed if there was any risk involved at all.

I decided I must go to bed. By now it was about two or three in the morning for me, but although I was tired I could not sleep. I thought of the many telephone calls between London and New York, and how Jack had rung me excitedly, saying he was not going to return home, but was staying to have the operation.

I recalled my protests and his reassurances that he had seen film, and heard tapes of people's voices who had already had the Voicbak installed; what it had done for them, it could do for him. But always it was with absolute firmness—'It is my own decision,' he said. I pleaded, should I not join him in New York? But he replied that there was nothing I could do while he was in hospital. It was not a serious operation, and it would be better for me to come during his recovery time. And so I stayed in London.

Then I thought of that other sleepless night—my heavens, there have been so many!—when I had decided I must have a final word with Jack before he undertook such a drastic step. The fact that he'd had cobalt treatment all those years ago, and the knowledge that this could make healing difficult, was uppermost in my mind, so I booked a call to the Plaza Hotel in New York for nine o'clock in the morning, so that I would be sure of getting him—only to find he had checked out leaving no address.

After trying to track him down through various friends in New York, as a last resort I rang the Flower and Fifth Avenue Hospital just in time to learn that he had already undergone pre-medication. I was too late; everything was out of my hands.

I recalled the telephone ringing by my bedside very late the following night, and Dr Taub on the line from New York saying that they had discovered a primary growth on Jack's pharynx. They had successfully removed this, and in any case they did not consider it particularly serious.

The news shocked me and the questions came tumbling out.

'Is he all right? His health was very good when he left for New York. Will this affect his future speech?'

But, most important, surely they would not now consider proceeding with the second operation to install the Voicbak? Should not Jack come home to see his own doctors first?

Dr Taub replied that, after consultation with specialists there, they intended to proceed, but I would not be able to talk to Jack and it was Jack's express wish that I should stay at home, as we had arranged, until the time came for him to leave hospital.

And so I was left to wait in London, growing more worried as the days went by without news from New York. When I got really frantic I would telephone friends there who would try to extract information, but this was virtually impossible, apart from the usual hospital clichés, 'He is as well as can be expected'.

Finally, our friend and lawyer in New York, Arnold Weiss-berger, and Jack's agent, Milton Goldman, were permitted to visit him and telephoned me with reassuring news.

Sleep that night in New York came to me at last, but only fit-fully, and by six o'clock in the morning I found myself wandering around Betty's apartment again, creeping so as not to disturb the baby and labrador. I made myself some tea and went and stood in the library looking over Central Park. It was Easter Sunday, the trees were coming into bud and it all looked so hopeful and bright. Perhaps this is how it was going to be for us as well? I wished I could convince myself.

I thought about the night before I left for New York, when I had a telephone call from Evelyn—at one time Sister Thorburn of St George's Hospital Maternity Ward, where both Nick and Andy were born. Although we had met only rarely over the years since, we have a close affinity—understandably, because she saved Nick's life after a very traumatic birth.

Therefore I was amazed but delighted to hear her voice, because she is married and no longer lives in London. She said she had read about Jack going to New York for the operation and ex-pressed interest and concern for me.

I told her I was off to America in the morning, and then she told me she had had an extraordinary dream which no doubt promp-ted her to telephone me. She dreamt I was standing on the top of a tall building that was swaying and crumbling and calling for her and saying, 'Evelyn, please help me. Everything is collapsing beneath me.'

She said this was so vivid that she could not get it out of her mind. I suppose I could have said something like that whilst Nicky was being born, but now, as I stood in the silent library, I remembered her describing this dream. She is a highly skilled member of the medical profession, and not a woman to be

161

influenced by dreams—or nightmares. Once more I had this uneasy sensation of impending disaster, and indeed that everything was beginning to fall away, out of my control.

The apartment began to stir for, with a young child, nobody sleeps late, and then we were in the kitchen making tea and all kinds of breakfasts. The Bogart family told me they were going to have lunch with Betty's stepfather and then on their various ways.

I was expecting Jack to be brought back, so I got things ready for him. He came at midday with Dr Stanley Taub, and it was wonderful to see his pleasure at being with me again and out of the hospital atmosphere. By this time it was a very warm day and we watched all the comings and goings in Central Park, the hot-dog stands, the Easter parades going through, and life seemed very good.

I soon mastered the intricacies of feeding Jack through the tube in his neck. This involved pouring watered-down baby food through a funnel connected by a long pipe to the tube in his neck. To let it run down, I had to stand on the kitchen table for, although I am tall, I wasn't tall enough. Although this didn't give either of us much pleasure it gave us a lot of laughs. Jack's wonderful sense of humour never deserted him.

Certainly, the mess I was pouring in didn't give him much enjoyment, and he was permanently hungry. Happily, in a few days, I was able to cook him some eggs, buy Italian food and wine from around the corner and life took on a rosier hue.

We were also able to see some friends. These included dear Raymond Massey, who was luckily in town, Christopher Plummer and his wife, Jamie, the younger son of David Niven, who has been my friend since he was two years old. They would drop by for a drink, and this was a great diversion for Jack and for me. Constance McIndoe, the widow of Sir Archibald McIndoe, the famous plastic surgeon, a close friend of many years, was in New York at that time—and how lucky I was to have her near me I was subsequently to discover.

At the end of the week, we managed to go out to dinner with

Connie and a friend, at the famous 21 Club, where we were given an incredible reception—understandably, because Jack had been going there since he was eighteen when he was in *Journey's End*. We have been there together many times over the years. The first time I was in New York with Jack in 1950 he took me there and I remember the fun I had in being shown the famous backroom where all the illegal stills were kept during the prohibition days.

But nothing in our previous visits compared with this night. In fact, as Connie laughingly remarked, since all the attention was being focused on Jack, she and I might just as well not have been there! This was good for his morale because it was quite evident to me—if to no one else—that he still was far from well.

The same thing happened the next day, when we went to the Plaza Hotel for lunch; people crowded around to wish him good luck and to shake his hand. Jack had always been amazingly popular in America. They admired him as an actor, for what he was as much as who he was, and what he represented: a straight, uncompromising way of behaviour. Now, they admired him for his courage.

During this time Dr Taub was waiting for the wound in Jack's neck to heal sufficiently to install the device, the Voicbak. Meanwhile, he had experimented on one occasion with a temporary mechanism and the result was quite dramatic. There was no doubt that it gave Jack much more vocal power and more breath control. For example, he could count up to thirty or forty without gulping, and spoke to me once on the telephone from Dr Taub's office with amazing clarity.

But the wound did not heal.

Instead, it seemed to me to be suppurating more than ever, and I was conscious of a strange odour which I could not pin down for a while, but which unlocked some memory in my mind. Suddenly, I had a vision of myself in Secunderabad in India, during the war, visiting hospital wards; over everything had hung this same smell. It came from infected wounds. I do not think that Jack was conscious of this, but I don't know, because we only ever talked optimistically together.

However, at the weekend the condition grew very much worse and, on Connie's advice, I called in both doctors who made some adjustments to the tube in Jack's neck, and reassured me that all was well. I did suggest that perhaps it was unwise to push on with the installation of the Voicbak until Jack was completely ready.

I knew that they were anxious, for many reasons, to achieve completion of the operation, and there was talk of teams of doctors being flown in to watch it, and even a documentary film being made.

Obviously, there was much interest and anticipation from the medical profession and also from the Press. In addition, Jack had work to do on a film, and we didn't want to extend our stay in New York any longer than necessary, but it seemed to me that my husband's health was more important than any of these considerations; in fact Jack himself felt this and both Dr Taub and Dr Bergner agreed.

Alas, there was no decision necessary because, while we were alone, getting ready for bed on the Monday night, the most frightening thing happened! Jack began to haemorrhage from the incision where the temporary tube was connected to his neck.

In a frantic state, I telephoned the doctors, but both were unobtainable. However, I got some good advice from Dr Taub's wife, who suggested I should apply ice-packs to stop the bleeding.

Dr Taub had been out at a medical dinner. When he returned home, he immediately telephoned me and I was able to tell him that I had stopped the bleeding. But in the middle of the night it started again and became uncontrollable, so I frantically rang Dr Taub once more, and he said he would be right over. Meanwhile he advised me to remove the tube and apply pressure to the neck. It's amazing what you can do when you have to, but I was utterly thankful when he arrived. He immediately realised that we could not cope between us and telephoned for an ambulance, which arrived with a police escort.

When you are in New York you hear police and ambulance sirens screaming all the time, now suddenly the sirens were screaming for us and the apartment was full of policemen, nurses and stretcher bearers. Then they were rushing Jack off, with Dr Taub holding his neck all the time, and I was left standing there, shaking like a leaf.

A nice New York cop turned to me.

'Don't you want to come, miss?' he asked.

Miss! I looked at myself with my hair hanging down and my nightgown covered in blood, and said: 'Thank you, no. I will just have some tea.'

After the chaos there was an awful silence and emptiness, and I walked along the corridor back to the bedroom. What a sight it was—like an abattoir. What to do but make the tea, and wait until seven o'clock—it was then about half past five—when I could ring Connie. We have always been so lucky in our friends, but how marvellous to have one who just jumps in a taxi and comes over immediately! She hardly left my side from then onwards. Certainly, I needed her, for the rest was all a nightmare.

Jack had a second haemorrhage after they had given him three pints of blood, and finally, late that night, Stanley Taub rang me from the hospital to say they had been forced to tie off the main carotid artery which had presumably given way with the infection.

Connie and I were sitting together in Betty's library, still looking at Central Park, when Dr Taub arrived, not having eaten all day. I made some sandwiches, and he told us how he had received the emergency call about the second haemorrhage when he was in his consulting rooms with a lady who was being examined for a bosom build-up (one of his specialities). He left her half naked on the couch, and leapt out into Fifth Avenue, white coat flapping, stethoscope dangling, and flagged down the nearest car to take him to the Flower and Fifth Avenue Hospital. This gave us a much needed laugh.

He was very unhappy—as, of course, we all were—sitting in a miserable group, trying to console each other, for Taub was desperately worried about Jack, and the realisation that it would now be virtually impossible to install the Voicbak on which he had placed such high hopes—not only for him, but for the many

165

others in the same situation who would take heart if Jack's operation were successful. I could only think of my husband.

Hospital visiting in New York is no easier than it is anywhere else. The Flower and Fifth Avenue is up on 106th Street, on the border of Harlem. From the West Side you have to cross the Park so it is almost impossible by public transport. Thus, morning and evening visits by walking and taxi consume your whole day.

Jack was bitterly unhappy and very depressed. He hated being in the Intensive Care Unit—understandably so, for there was no rest or peace. Thus, when, after five days, they decided to move him back to a private room, I felt very relieved. This must be an indication that he was getting better, and with that thought in mind I allowed myself to be taken out for lunch with Connie and a mutual friend, Shirley Lord. We didn't linger over it and rushed on to the hospital afterwards, stopping only to buy the English newspapers for Jack.

We hurried along the seventh-floor corridor again, Connie full of optimism, and me still tentative. I went to kiss Jack and found him looking ashen, more ill than I had seen him look the entire time. Frightened, I went back into the corridor and cannoned into Doctors Taub and Bergner, who had quite obviously been talking seriously to Connie whom I could see in the distance watching me with a very grave expression on her face.

'What is the matter? What is happening?' I demanded, but I could tell by the look in their eyes that it was something awful. I backed up against the wall, because there were no seats anywhere and they stood, one on either side of me. Their sentences came through to me only dimly, but I did realise I had to make a decision very quickly. An immediate operation had to be performed to save his life. A blood clot had formed where the artery had been tied off, so really there was no decision to make.

Connie said later I looked like a stag at bay. I only remember my knees giving way and sliding down the wall and being heaved up again. In the idiotic way one's mind goes off at a tangent, I remembered my days of playing in farce, and the male actors doing this very expertly in drunk scenes. Come to think of it,

166

I suppose my training as an actress has been a great asset; it has certainly helped me to present a good face to the world through many difficult years.

Connie and I came out into Fifth Avenue, gulped fresh air, and then went back to Betty's apartment for the long wait. Seven hours of vascular surgery with a vein graft and were we not lucky—if one can use this word—to have one of America's most eminent vascular surgeons in the Flower and Fifth on that particular day?

At one o'clock on the following morning, after many enquiries, when I was told my husband was still on the operating table, I finally had news. The operation had apparently been successful. He would live.

Although I had many friends in New York, they were mostly working in the theatre, and my life was completely bound up with Jack and visiting the hospital, so when Connie had to return to England I was suddenly desperately alone. I was obviously not in the frame of mind to get dressed up and go out to a party, and New York seemed such a different city. I remembered the time when, on the opposite side of the Park, Jack and I had Ty Power's apartment, a little penthouse on 72nd Street. Jack was working on *Caesar and Cleopatra* for television, and we were wonderfully happy there—except when it snowed so hard he had to walk all the way downtown, being passed by sensible people SKIING along Fifth Avenue, a sight I shall never forget.

And then, of course, the brilliant first night of *Bridge on the River Kwai*. Ty and Jack did a TV reception before it and Sam Spiegel gave an unforgettable party afterwards that lasted until dawn.

We had known so much happiness right here in New York, but now I was desolate and walking around Betty's apartment on my own, in and out of the rooms, looking at all her photographs and pictures and possessions—so personal that they helped me. But suddenly, I realised, this was not enough.

On impulse, I picked up the telephone, rang our eldest son, Nicholas, in England, and told him to come over and join me. He was waiting and ready, and arrived two days later. Together, we got Jack out of hospital and nursed him back into sufficient health to bring him home to England. And never in all my life was I so thankful to get home.

Our departure from the airport had been almost gay. We had friends to see us off, the airline provided hospitality, Jack was more like his old self, joking with everyone and signing autographs. He was still rather weak, however, for apart from the frightful loss of blood, he had been on a miserable diet for so many weeks.

It seemed unbelievable that I had been in New York for so long. The trees, just in bud at Easter, were now in full leaf. Betty had sung and danced her way through many performances of *Applause* in London whilst all the dramas had taken place in her apartment.

On the flight home, Jack slept most of the time, while Nick and I whispered to one another across the aisle. I was sorry that he had seen so little of New York. It had been his first visit, and I would dearly have loved to show him around. He had many invitations, but he refused them all, saying he'd come over to be with us and to help his father.

And what a help he was! He is like Jack in build, but even bigger and very strong. He also possesses a great gift for seeing the funny side of everything, and his wit is very sharp and amusing, so his presence in what had been an atmosphere of prevailing gloom brought in a gleam of light. We both delighted in his company. Also, it meant I had to cook some food—previously, when on my own, I would eat bananas, for no preparation was necessary, and they are so easy to swallow; or I would grab something from the fridge. Occasionally, if I had time, Betty's maid would make me a quick salad. But with Nick and, at last, Jack home from hospital, I had to think about food—which was just as well, for I'd become as thin as a rake.

Nick and I talked quietly about Jack's proposed stay in East Grinstead Hospital. Partly through Connie McIndoe and other good friends associated with the Queen Victoria Hospital, they kindly offered to have him in for physiotherapy and a general tone-up. As he was due to start work fairly soon, this seemed an excellent idea. Also, if any plastic surgery was needed to close the fistula in his neck, the best surgeons in the land were there to carry it out.

So, after a marvellous welcome home—oh, how good it was to see it again, filled with flowers and the warmth of family and friendship!—Jack went to East Grinstead for two weeks.

Their kind attention certainly showed very soon in his appearance, for he looked fitter and quite brown, because he spent a lot of time in the hospital grounds. But, sadly, they could do nothing about the wound, which was still open. A friend, the plastic surgeon, explained to me that the infection still existed, in spite of all the antibiotics that had been pumped into Jack, both in New York and now in England. Cultures had been grown and various new prescriptions were tried to kill this virulent bug—but all without success.

This worried Jack greatly, for not only was the wound causing him discomfort, but having to wear a dressing over his neck made it difficult for him to wear a suit and collar and tie. He discussed this problem with the costume designer of the film company when he went for his clothes fitting for *The Tamarind Seed*, but they found some way round it, and soon Jack was busy learning his lines and looking forward so much to working again; this was his life and he was never happier than when filming.

Julie Andrews was the star with Omar Sharif, our old friend from *Lawrence of Arabia* days. Jack was to start shooting at Pinewood which, for him, was like going home. Only one or two days were scheduled, and then to Paris for a short location.

I did not have any doubts that he would make it and that work would be the best therapy in the world. Afterwards, a film in Africa was planned. Life began to look more normal and less like a nightmare, and I felt some of the strain and worry of the past weeks beginning to fall from me.

But what we all hoped for was not to be. We had not seen Andrew, our younger son, for some weeks, because he was at Chichester Festival Theatre. He was there as a student, helping to shift the scenery and generally make himself useful. After Oxford, he had been on an olive farm in Italy, enjoying the open-air life and perfecting his Italian, but he had always had a strong leaning towards the theatre and this was a splendid way to make a start.

On the Sunday of June 10 we were to celebrate his birthday. He would arrive for Sunday lunch and we were all looking forward to it immensely. Nick, by this time, had returned to his job out of London. On the Sunday morning, Jack was about to take a bath and I was in the adjoining bedroom, dressing, when I heard a strangled cry, which was all too horribly familiar. I rushed into the bathroom to find him pouring blood, just as in New York.

Panic and horror at the sight. I was alone as before—Caroline had gone out to play tennis. What to do first? Try to stop the bleeding, ring a doctor, or get Jack to lie down?

Quickly, the telephone in my bedroom. My hands were shaking so much that I couldn't dial the number and, of course, got a wrong one. When I got through, it was our doctor's wife who answered: he was, of course, out visiting patients and his brother was on holiday. She told me to waste no time and dial 999, which I did and, thank God, the response was immediate.

I explained my desperate need and then rushed back to Jack. He was standing there, trembling with the fearful effort of applying pressure to his neck to stop the spurting blood. I managed somehow to get him into the bedroom and flat on the bed, and draped him in towels. Remembering New York, I rushed for ice from the fridge and packed the cubes around the wound.

I suppose the ambulance was about fifteen minutes arriving but, as during that dreadful night in Betty's apartment, it seemed an eternity.

Somehow, between us, Jack and I had more or less stopped the bleeding. You learn very quickly the hard way. Then everything seemed too horribly familiar: I had been here before, with the stretchers, the attendants, being so gentle and kind and I, half-dressed. This time, I flung on some trousers and a sweater and went along in the ambulance to St Stephen's Hospital in Fulham Road. Jack was calm and so brave, as always, but I knew what his thoughts must be; very much the same as mine.

Our doctor had been hooked off his round and he joined us at the hospital. I was grateful for his reassuring presence. In the last twenty-five years, we have been through many situations together —good and bad.

I thanked heaven that I had insisted on being given as much information as possible before we left the medical team in New York. And so I took Jack's medical dossier with me in the ambulance, for the mysteries of the operation performed on Jack, and the subsequent complications involving the vascular surgery, presented St Stephen's with vast and unknown problems.

Many discussions—but at least the haemorrhaging had ceased, and as I held Jack's hand, his only thought was that I must let the film company know as soon as possible, so that they could re-cast. Then I remembered Andy. He would be arriving home for his birthday at any moment, so I went back to the silence and the cleaning up, as I had done once before. To keep myself occupied after this, I started to prepare some food, so when the doorbell rang, I hoped I was looking very much myself.

However, when Andrew saw my face, he said: 'Something's happened. I knew it, driving back.'

Poor Andy. It was hardly a birthday celebration. Later, I took him to see his father but, by this time, Jack had been moved to a room on the top floor and, lying in bed, still with his suntan, he looked well, appeared to be relaxed, but was naturally depressed by the disasters of the morning, and particularly about missing his film.

During the following week, Jack was inundated with presents and letters from his many friends and admirers; his spirits seemed high, and he was cared for so well. The main problem was this dreadful infection, and the hated and painful injections that punctuated the day for him. I did my best to provide reasonably palatable food, for he was allowed very little by mouth. Just as I was beginning to feel a small wave of optimism again, another crisis occurred: that telephone call at 1 a.m. waking me in a second, heart thumping. Would I go over as soon as possible? Another emergency.

171

I was in the car within ten minutes, and driving to Fulham Road. I arrived in the ward just in time to see Jack being wheeled, covered in blood, to the lift, surrounded by many people in white coats and masks. I managed to push through them to kiss him, and he gave me a wink and forced a smile. Then they all disappeared and my knees began to give way, but this time there was a seat. I flopped thankfully into it. Later I wandered towards his room, where the nurses were busy cleaning up. They barred the way so that I could not see the blood, and suggested kindly that I should wait until they had finished. I replied dully that I had seen it all before.

That was the longest night for me. I walked the hospital corridors, out into the car park, back again, and then sat in the car, watching the dawn come up. It was so beautiful that somehow I was certain in my heart that Jack would not live to see it. But he did. At seven o'clock that morning, I was back in the Sister's room, and they rang from the operating theatre to say that the carotid artery had been tied off yet again, and they had won the battle.

But it was becoming obvious to me that nobody was confident that this was the end of the story. Indeed, a pattern began to emerge. After about ten days, just as soon as everyone thought that the infection in the fistula had been controlled, the dreadful bleeding would begin again.

Nick had moved back to London to be with me and at one stage hopes ran high enough for me to go away. My own doctor, and also the doctors in St Stephen's, said that I must have a break and so, leaving Nick in charge, I flew down to our house in France. I left with many misgivings, but apart from the rest I so badly needed, many matters there were calling for my attention, for we had not been near the villa since the previous September. But it was a wasted journey. I spent one night there, and had barely unpacked, when Nick rang for me to return immediately. It had happened again; another haemorrhage.

I got myself on a night flight and was in St Stephen's by one o'clock in the morning. Nick was waiting for me, having endured the long wait just as I had done many times. He put his arms around me and led me into the Intensive Care Unit where his father lay and, although Jack was weak, when I kissed him he whispered that I should not have come back from France.

From then on, there was a slow deterioration although, at times, Jack seemed so much better, one hoped that perhaps, in spite of everything, he might recover. He was a strong, brave man, with a great desire to get on with life.

One evening, after the final haemorrhage, when the necessary pressure had been applied to the artery, he appeared to be relapsing more and more into a comatose state between sleep and wakefulness. Nick and I drove home together, facing the inevitable; the end now could only be a matter of time, and measured in hours rather than days.

I asked Nick: 'How am I going to live without this man?'

'Mother,' he replied. 'You and Dad had the most wonderful marriage, and enjoyed a happiness that most people never find. Many never know what it's all about.'

Of course he was right, and how comforting it was to hear it from him.

The news came through at one o'clock in the morning: 'Your husband died at ten past twelve.'

Although it was anticipated, I froze completely; it was as though a part of me had also died.

Caroline, Nick and I lay in a heap on my bed holding hands, trying to keep me warm although it was a hot night. This was the same bed where Caroline was born, the only baby I had at home.

I thought of that—happy days—sun streaming in my bedroom window through the trees; a gorgeous September day, and I had produced a daughter. I could hear Jack's joyous shouts. He was kissing everyone in the house and champagne corks were popping. I hoped someone would bring me some! I need not have worried; Jack was in as soon as he was allowed. Tea? No, I didn't want tea, I would have a sip out of his glass.

He adored our two boys, but I always knew he longed for a

daughter. Maybe it was something to do with missing Sue's childhood? Sue—my God—we have to let her know.

Nick cabled her in California. She had had a little warning, but not much. Then Andy—how to reach him? We did not want him to hear the news first from someone else. We missed having him with us, and he would need us perhaps, and it would be wrong if he heard such news on the radio or read it on a placard. Then we suddenly realised we had no address—he had just changed digs. Send a telegram to the Chichester Theatre, that's all. He had been so upset when he had seen his father on Sunday. He must have guessed it would be the last time, and he was trying so hard to get through to him. I think he succeeded.

I am so cold. We all are. Nick fetched some brandy, and we sipped it between us and comforted ourselves that at least he would not suffer any more, and we would not have to watch his despair and unhappiness.

Jack has found his quiet life. Now I have to try and find mine.

DOREEN HAWKINS
*July* 1973

# INDEX